WebPlus 10 User Guide

How to Contact Us

Our main office (UK, Europe):

The Software Centre
PO Box 2000, Nottingham, NG11 7GW, UK

Main	(0115) 914 2000
Registration (UK only)	(0800) 376 1989
Sales (UK only)	(0800) 376 7070
Technical Support (UK only)	(0845) 345 6770
Customer Service (UK only)	(0845) 345 6770
Customer Service/ Technical Support (International)	+44 115 914 9090
General Fax	(0115) 914 2020
Technical Support e-mail	**support@serif.co.uk**

American office (USA, Canada):

The Software Center
13 Columbia Drive, Suite 5, Amherst, NH 03031

Main	(603) 889-8650
Registration	(800) 794-6876
Sales	(800) 55-SERIF or 557-3743
Technical Support	(603) 886-6642
Customer Service	(800) 489-6720
General Fax	(603) 889-1127
Technical Support e-mail	**support@serif.com**

Online

Visit us on the Web at	**http://www.serif.com**
Serif newsgroups	**news://news.serif.com**

International

Please contact your local distributor/dealer. For further details please contact us at one of our phone numbers above.

Comments or other feedback

We want to hear from you! Please e-mail **feedback@serif.com** with your ideas and comments, or use the Serif Web forums!

Contents

Welcome

1

Welcome to **WebPlus 10.0** from **Serif**—still the easiest way ever to get your business, organization, or household on the World Wide Web!

Whether you're a new WebPlus user, or have upgraded from a previous edition, you're sure to appreciate the range of powerful features we've included. As always, if you have comments or suggestions—or samples of the work you create with WebPlus—we'd like to hear from you.

And don't forget to register your new copy, using the Serif Registration Wizard. That way, we can keep you informed of new developments and future upgrades.

What's New in WebPlus 10...

The focus in WebPlus 10 is very much on opening up WebPlus to allow it to be used as a platform for developing dynamic web pages—making modern fast-moving content packed full of interest! Advanced web users gain by being able to edit HTML source code directly. Let's look at the new WebPlus 10 features in turn.

- **E-Commerce—Sell, Sell, Sell!** (p. 199)
  WebPlus makes the process of placing items for sale on your web site quick and easy with its built-in support for E-Commerce shopping cart providers (e.g., **PayPal**)! Simply adding E-Commerce Forms, E-Commerce Buttons, or even a hyperlink from any WebPlus object (text, pictures or shapes) will access your chosen shopping cart. **Buy Now**, **Add to Shopping Cart**, **Donation**, and **Subscription** forms will get money moving with buying options and form validation thrown in! Sign up to shopping carts directly or adopt existing accounts.

- **Web-ready Forms for gathering content** (p. 172)
  Apply forms to your web pages—use a WebForm Wizard to adopt ready-to-go standard forms for **contact details**, **user feedback/comments**, **canvassing opinions**, or **uploading documents** (e.g., CVs) or pictures. Use **Standard Form Objects** as building blocks to slash form design time! Submit form data via Web Resources, Serif's free form-to-email transit gateway (data goes straight to your email on submission) or subject data to local/remote scripting. Control tab order for improved form navigation.

- **Send Current Page as E-mail** (p. 65)
  Create fantastic looking HTML email with WebPlus's outstanding layout capabilities. Send your page design as an **advertising email link**, use for **web site launches**, or **promote you products** and **services**!

- **Serif Web Resources for FREE!** (p. 188)
  Add rich dynamic content using Smart Objects such as **blogs**, **page counters**, **polls**, and more, to make your web site a truly interactive experience. Serif Web resources also allows you to manage your blogs from anywhere in the world—simply log on to ... **Serif Web Resources**.

- **Photo Gallery** (p. 141)
  Run a photo-rich web site using the WebPlus **Photo Gallery**. Share online albums of family, special occasions, or personal photo collections. Various thumbnailed gallery types are provided (in thumbnail grid, strips or bars) with click-to-view image control—each type is fully navigable and, or course, good on the eye. Decorative **frames**, **shadows**, **glows**, **caption** support, custom **filter effects**, and **image adjustments** complement any Photo Gallery. All the common photo formats are supported, as is the **automatic rotation** of digital-camera photos.

- **Great Creative Content!**
  Webplus comes with a fantastic range of **pre-built samples**, **templates** and **gallery** items to fast track your way to impressive web sites. Take advantage of the dynamic Flash™ banners incorporated in templates to give that cutting edge look. Easily customize them with WebPlus's extensive support for passing parameters to flash objects.

- **RSS—News and Information Feeds on your page** (p. 194)
  Keep your web visitors up to date with the latest news from your favourite websites (BBC News, Reuters, FTSE, NASDAQ) with the **RSS Reader Tool**. Alternatively, be a news anchor yourself by creating your own RSS feed directly on your page—the **RSS Feed Tool** sets up feeds, headlines, summaries and URL links.

- **HTML-Compatible Frames and Tables** (p. 70 and 93)
  Design frames and tables based on **HTML**! Take advantage of HTML's heading tags to get your web site noticed in your web visitor's favourite search engines.

- **Split you page into Frames!** (p. 42)
  Scrolling frame support is now brought to your WebPlus project with the **Framed Document Tool**. Add a framed menu or navigation frame or view page-in-page with multiple frames in the same browser window.

- **Attach code to objects—add HTML and script!** (p. 166)
  Apply **HTML code** to objects, table cells, HTML fragments and complete pages—apply scripts (with embedded or linked supporting files) to increase user interaction. Insert **tokens** as dynamic placeholders to include dates, colours, page titles, file names, etc. Auto-generate HTML IDs for any object to allow JavaScript manipulation. Interested in getting down to HTML basics? Develop **raw HTML pages**, all navigable via WebPlus's Site Structure.

- **Enhanced Import HTML** (p. 24)
  Now **Import Web pages** with accompanying meta data, server-side script, JavaScript, hotspots, and forms!

- **Manage by file and folder structure!** (p. 61)
  Use **File Manager** to manage your web site. View underlying folder structures, create your own folders, add different file types and rename from within WebPlus.

- **Play and Manipulate Shockwave Flash Files** (p. 138)
  WebPlus gives you the ability to see your flash animations and play them within the design view. We have also provided professionally designed flash banners which you can customize.

- **Onboard Image adjustments** (p. 133)
  Benefit from "on-board" image adjustments for **quick colour correction** of imported images and objects converted to pictures—pick from Auto Levels, Auto Contrast, Brightness/Contrast, Channel Mixer, Colour Balance, Curves, and many more. Commonly used **special effects** such as Diffuse Glow, Dust and Scratch Remover, Shadows/Highlights, and various blurs make up the set of adjustments, which can be applied in combination. You can now eliminate the dreaded red eye effect on subjects in your photos with the new **Red Eye Tool** with a single click. If you want to do even more, use the handy **Edit in PhotoPlus** option (version 10 or above) from within WebPlus to edit and save images and PhotoPlus files with impressive synergy.

- **Context Toolbars**
  WebPlus now supports context toolbars which host tool options and settings that dynamically change according to the currently selected object or tool used in your drawing. Only the necessary tool settings and options are at hand for edit or reference, speeding up the design process while making the user experience easier.

- **New User Interface**
WebPlus has undergone major rework to ensure all the content you need is always at your fingertips. A whole series of **dockable Studio tabs** now replace the Studio toolbar and ChangeBar available in previous WebPlus versions. These provide single-click access to commonly used settings such as Line, Opacity, and Colour. More precise control is also possible when aligning objects (**Align tab**), formatting text (**Character tab**) and positioning objects (**Transform tab**). A Swatches tab hosts a myriad of palette-based colour swatches for solid, gradient and bitmap fills and line colouration—you can even add, view, edit or delete colours you have been using in your web site from within the Publication palette. The existing Site tab has been revitalized with an optional preview/layout mode.

  Every tab can be docked/undocked, grouped with other tabs, resized in any direction or shown/hidden. You can also create different configurations of these tabs and save them as **separate workspaces** for instant recall whenever you wish. Collapse tabs in a specific order according to usage.

- **Enhanced FTP Upload!** (p. 211)
New FTP features include uploading your WebPlus project to safeguard against loss. Manually control which files to upload during more versatile incremental updates. Fancy a fresh start? Now delete the entire site in one operation.

- **Font Control** (p. 63)
Use **WebSafe Fonts Manager** to standardize fonts between your web site and your target audiences' computers. Define any font as WebSafe or force rasterization. Planning to use a third-party WebPlus project? Avoid problems with missing fonts by using the Resource Manager's **font substitution** capabilities.

- **..and some very useful additions you've been asking for!**
  Master Page objects now **Attach to Bottom to Page** when expanding a web page's height. Link to remote Internet-hosted pictures to build-up your page content quickly. Swap your currently placed image between different format quickly and easily—GIF to PNG (or JPG), or any combination (also alter bit depth, transparency and/or size/resolution. A new **Colour tab** offers colour tinting and different colour display modes. New page properties include extra settings for more powerful page retrieval in **search engines** (e.g., use of language codes), **Page Redirect**, **Estimate Download Time**, and **Page Transitions**—pick from spirals, circles, blinds, wipe effects, and many more! Use **Paste In Place** and **Paste Format** as new object editing options. **Navigation bars** are now customizable for added flexibility. **Auto-save** on publish and preview (or by time interval), and product **Auto-update** are new options. **Java applets** loaded direct from JAR or ZIP (no extraction needed). A new **active hyperlinks scheme** is added. Output your site with different **HTML encoding**: UTF-8, windows-1252, or ISO 8859-1. Include your web site's icon (e.g., a company logo) in your visitor's browser favourites. Import Serif **PhotoPlus .SPP** files and **Photoshop .PSD** files (with clipped paths). And last but not least… enhancements to **Find & Replace**, **Guide lines**, **Animated Marquees**, **Master Page Manager** and **Web Export Options (**image format conversion on export, JPG quality, resampling, and optimization) round off the exciting WebPlus 10**!**

Plus these established WebPlus features..

- **Navigation by Page and Site Structure**
  The **Site Structure tree** not only serves as a control centre for manipulating pages, it helps you visually arrange your pages into a hierarchy of sections and levels... think like an architect as you design a sensible content layout! Browse pages quickly from the HintLine toolbar. Easily customize a host of properties for individual pages: Length, background colour, centring, file name, title, and more. Import HTML Web pages, even entire sites.

- **Importing and Editing**
  For text, you can import, paste, export in **Unicode** format... design with foreign-language or exotic/symbol fonts and characters. Use drag-and-drop editing in WritePlus. Clear formatting (revert to plain style) with a single keystroke.

  For pictures, import images at 96dpi screen resolution. Adjust brightness and contrast, size and resolution, apply colouration and view properties with the Picture context toolbar. Add any workspace colour to the palette with a single click. Import **Flash** (.SWF) animated movies or **MP3** audio files!

- **Page Anchors and Hyperlink Improvements**
  You can insert **anchors** to target hyperlinks directly to any word or onscreen object... Automatically link downsized "thumbnail" images to full-sized versions on an empty page... Open links in a new window as needed... Include **offsite links** in your site structure... Convert hotspots to match selected shapes.

- **Theme Graphics for Instant Flair**
  Choose from an array of **ready-made design elements** in themed sets, on a Theme Graphics tab... Swap sets and change the look of your site with a single click... Customize text, font, colours, and more. Intelligent theme graphics like **navigation bars** and Previous/Next buttons are programmed to reflect your site structure... adapt automatically as you rearrange pages. Effortlessly establish easy-to-follow pathways throughout your site!

- **Animated Marquees**
  Add life to your Web pages! Custom-design your own varied and colourful **multi-line text messages** that scroll across the screen... Add your own responsive buttons with the multi-layered **Rollover graphics** option.

- **Versatile Web Feature Support**
  WebPlus supports current HTML for better WYSIWYG page design. Add **sound** and **video**—even **Java** and HTML header/body code—to spice up your pages! The Layout Checker helps you fine-tune your site before it's published. Then preview your site in your own Web browser and publish it to a local folder or a remote server.

- **Enveloping**
  Apply a customizable mesh warp envelope to any object to add perspective, slant, bulge, and more. You can deform just the outline or include the object's fill, with an optional grid revealing the geometry of your warp.

- **Intelligent Colour Schemes**
  Choose from dozens of preset **colour schemes** to change the overall appearance of your Web site with a single click. You can customize the scheme colours, create brand new schemes, and apply any scheme to a "from-scratch" site.

- **Object Styles Transform with a Single Click**
  Select any object (including text) and choose from a gallery of **ready-made styles** that combine a host of attributes such as 3D filter effects, fills, transparency, line styles, border—even font variations. Customize the preset styles or create your own!

- **On-screen Studio Combines Convenience with Functionality**
  Floatable, dockable Studio tabs provide rapid drag-and-drop access to commonly-used controls such as fonts, line settings, and the colour table. Use the **Gallery** to store your favourite designs for use in any Web site... with built-in flashes, logos, and lots of other page elements you can customize to suit your needs!

- **Professional Layout and Text Tools**
  Intelligent text fitting. Movable rulers and guides. Precision placement, rotation, flipping, cropping, vertical alignment. The Replicate tool to multiply any object into a line or grid arrangement, with pinpoint control over offset and spacing. Text formatting with **named styles**. Multiple **master pages** for repeating background elements. Not to mention word count, search and replace, spell-checking with personal dictionary, thesaurus, and proof reader to ensure your site's readability.

- **Artistic Text Tool**
  Complementing traditional text in frames, just **click and type anywhere** on the page, format with the customary tools, then apply colourful lines and fills directly at the character level. Scale it, rotate it, flip it... discover a host of new possibilities! **Path text tools** let you draw your line, and start typing... beautiful text flows along the path. You can edit the path as any line (altering the text flow accordingly) and still change the text properties at any time!

- **Table Tool with Editable Calendars**
  Create and edit tables right in your site, with no need for a separate utility. Choose from a range of preset formats or design your own by customizing lines, cells, rows, and columns. Powerful text manipulation features include AutoClear, AutoFill, and cell merge. Plus table-based **calendars**!

- **Amazing Image Manipulation**
  Import images inline as part of frame text flow, and create your own 32-bit anti-aliased TIFFs and PNGs. Convert to Picture allows instant, in-place format changes! Add **borders** to your imported pictures and shape art... even frame a text frame! Control imported metafiles and OLE options, maintain linked images... each export filter remembers its own settings.

- **QuickShapes**
  Long an exclusive feature of other Serif solutions, **QuickShapes** work like intelligent clipart... or the most powerful set of drawing tools you can imagine. Just choose a template shape, drag on the page... then adjust handles to customize each angle and dimension.

- **Powerful Drawing Options**
  An arsenal of drawing tools are at your command... Sketch **freehand lines and curves**. Extend existing lines with ease. Apply **line styles** to all kinds of shapes—even add line endings like arrowheads and diamonds. Use the Curve context toolbar to fine-tune the contours of any line, closed shape, or cropping edge. Sketch using calligraphic lines with an adjustable pen angle. Add rounded corners (caps) when and where you need them. Customize your lines using dots and dashes... vary the join style of connected lines.

- **Intelligent Bézier Curves**
  Now simply "connect the dots" to trace around curved objects and pictures... the improved Curved Line tool features **Smart segments** that use automatic curve-fitting to connect each node! Use Crop to Shape to trim one object to another... **Convert to Curves** for node-and-segment control over all objects, including QuickShapes.

- **Gradient and Bitmap Fills, Transparencies**
  For sophisticated illustrations and impressive typographic effects, select from a wide variety of Linear, Radial, and Conical fills and transparencies ...and a multi-faceted Studio gallery of picture-based effects. Use the interactive Fill and Transparency tools for drag-and-drop updating.

- **Striking Shadow, Glow, and Bevel Effects**
  One dialog serves as your "creation station," where you can select and preview a **spectacular range of special effects** for text or any object. Choose from soft-edged transparent Drop Shadow, Inner Shadow, Inner Glow, or Outer Glow, plus four Bevel and Emboss effects!

- **Astounding 3D Lighting and Surface Effects**
  Beyond the above 2D effects, **3D Filter Effects** now bring flat shapes to life! Choose one or more effects, then vary surface and source light properties. Start with a pattern or a function, adjust parameters for incredible surface contours, textures, fills—realistic-looking wood, water, skin, marble and much more.... The **feathering** filter effect adds a soft or blurry edge to any object. Great for blends, montages, vignetted photo borders, and much more.

- **Dramatic Dimensionality**
  Why settle for only two dimensions? **Instant 3D** adds realistic depth to ordinary objects and text. Use one master control panel to vary extrusion, rotation, bevel, lighting, texture, and more.

- **Web Preview**
  Use any window for an internal **Internet Explorer preview** of your site at configurable page sizes... or view external previews using **any browser** installed on your system

- **Total Ease-of-Use**
  Drag and drop objects from other applications. AutoScroll automatically adjusts your view as you move or resize. Right-click menus, HintLine, and context-sensitive cursors make WebPlus as friendly as a puppy!

About this User Guide

This User Guide focuses on information essential to the design, publishing and management of your web site. As a feature-rich product, WebPlus supports many more features which can't all be included in this User Guide. To assist, the following table lists some other books and topics exclusively available within the WebPlus Online Help. Scan the help's **Contents** for these books and topics for more information!

Online Help books	Topics covered in book...
How to Enhance Ease of Use	Customizing WebPlus toolbars and Studio tabs Setting WebPlus options Using shortcuts Using PageHints
How to Edit Objects on a Page	Selecting an object Selecting multiple objects Copying, pasting, and replicating objects Moving objects Resizing objects Rotating an object Flipping an object Cropping an object Applying mesh warp envelopes Locking an object's
How to Arrange Objects	Ordering objects Aligning objects Converting an object to a picture Exporting as picture Creating groups

How to Work with Colour, Fills and Transparency	Working with gradient and bitmap fills Managing colours and palettes Changing or copying vector image colours Working with transparency
How to Work with Lines, Shapes, and Effects	Setting line properties Applying shadows, glow, bevel, and emboss Using 3D filter effects Understanding blend modes Feathering Adding dimensionality (Instant 3D) Adding borders Using object styles
Misc Books	Basic Printing Editing Story Text with WritePlus

Registration, Upgrades, and Support

If you see the Registration Wizard when you launch WebPlus, please take a moment to complete the registration process. Follow the simple on-screen instructions and you'll be supplied a personalized registration number in return. If you need technical support please contact us, we aim to provide fast, friendly service and knowledgeable help. There's also a wide range of support information available 24 hours a day on our website at **www.serif.com**.

Installation

System Requirements

If you need help installing Windows, or setting up peripherals, see Windows documentation and help.

Minimum:

- Pentium PC with CD-ROM drive and mouse (or other Microsoft-compatible pointing device)
- Microsoft Windows® 98 SE, Me, 2000, or XP operating system
- 64MB RAM minimum
- 241MB (recommended install) free hard disk space
- SVGA (800x600 resolution, 16-bit colour) display or higher
- Internet Explorer 5.5 (6.0 for Windows 2000)

Additional disk resources and memory are required when editing large or complex documents.

Optional:

- Windows-compatible printer
- TWAIN-compatible scanner and/or digital camera
- Internet account and connection required for Publishing to Web and accessing online resources

First-time Install

To install WebPlus 10, simply insert the Program CD-ROM into your CD-ROM drive. The AutoRun feature automatically starts the Setup process and all you need to do is answer the on-screen questions. If the AutoRun does not start the install, use the manual install instructions below.

If you've also obtained the *WebPlus 10 Resource CD*, install it now following the same procedure you used for the Program CD.

Manual Install/Re-install

To re-install the software or to change any part of the installation at a later date, select **Control Panel** from the Windows **Start** menu (via the **Settings** item for pre-XP systems) and then double-click the **Add/Remove Programs** icon. Make sure the correct CD-ROM is inserted into your CD-ROM drive, choose **Serif WebPlus 10**, and click the **Install...** button. You'll have the choice of removing or adding components, re-installing components, or removing all components.

Getting Started

2

Understanding Web sites

This chapter and those that follow provide you with the details you'll need to know to create a successful site on the World Wide Web using WebPlus.

What's involved in creating a Web site?

It can be as simple as choosing and customizing a Web template... or you can start from scratch—it's up to you. Either way, you'll appreciate the ease with which WebPlus lets you revise text and graphics, and adjust the design of each page. WebPlus gives you the freedom to lay out page elements in any composition that suits you. It's a bit like putting together a newsletter—so if you're already comfortable with the basics of DTP, you'll find it easy going. If you're just beginning, you can learn to use WebPlus tools as you go.

WebPlus lets you assemble all the elements of your site-in-progress into one convenient, multi-page document that can be saved in a single step as a WebPlus **project file**. At any time—again with just one step—you can **publish** the project as a separate set of pages that comprise your **Web site**.

What exactly is a Web site?

The **Internet** is a global network that interconnects computers around the world. The **World Wide Web** began as a way of using the Internet to access information stored in a file format known as **HTML**, or Hypertext Markup Language. Broadly defined, a **Web site** is a collection of (mostly) HTML files stored on a **file server** that someone with a **Web browser** can get to. Actually, Web sites don't depend on the Internet at all—they can be (and often are) accessed just as well over a local area network or private intranet. Remember, a Web site is just a collection of files.

The HTML format is a way of describing the layout of a page. An HTML file uses plain text with various embedded codes to describe a page that somebody has designed, consisting of text and clickable hypertext links. Besides HTML files, a Web site generally includes other files (pictures, for example) that the designer has seen fit to incorporate. A Web browser such as Microsoft Internet Explorer or Netscape Navigator is a program that can read an HTML file and display the page (one hopes) the way the designer intended it to look.

Typically, a Web site has a single **Home Page** using a standard file name like INDEX.HTML. The Home Page is the first page a visitor sees. It usually will contain links to other pages on the site, which in turn have links to others. To the person using a Web browser to access the site, the information appears seamlessly linked—navigable with a click of the mouse.

WebPlus takes the pages you've laid out and converts them to HTML.

What will I need to preview or publish my Web site?

You can **preview** one or more pages at any time, either within WebPlus (using a special window based on the Internet Explorer browser) or separately using any browser installed on your system.

Publishing a site with WebPlus is a one-step operation that both: (1) converts your project to separate files for the Web, and (2) copies the Web files to a location you specify, either to a local folder or to a World Wide Web host.

- To publish to a **local folder**, you don't even need a connection to the Internet.

- To publish to the **World Wide Web**, you'll need a **host** for your Web site—that is, disk space on a server connected to the Internet—so that others can access your site. This usually means opening an account with an online service provider: either a large entity such as America Online or a specialized Internet service provider (ISP) . The big subscription networks typically allocate to each user several megabytes of server space for a "personal web site," and many plans are available from smaller ISPs. Once you've set up your account and can connect your computer to the host, publishing to the Web is simply a matter of transferring your files. The **Publish to Web** feature included with WebPlus takes care of this.

What about HTML?

One advantage WebPlus has over a dedicated Web-page creation program is that you can take your newsletter layout, or a print ad with a wild mix of multicolour graphics and fancy typography, and publish them intact to the World Wide Web. In fact, your page can look as great on the Web as it did on your screen!

While you don't have to know HTML (the description language for Web pages) to use WebPlus, you should understand that:

1. The time it takes a visitor to load your page is directly related to the size of the HTML file plus any accompanying graphic or multimedia files. These other files take up considerably more space—and slow down loading time.

2. Those parts of your layout that WebPlus cannot translate to HTML will be output as graphics. The more of your layout that WebPlus can translate into HTML, the better.

If you're used to working in a Desktop Publishing environment, you may have to scale back your typographic expectations somewhat when designing for the Web. However, WebPlus gives you a lot of design latitude. In laying out text, you can specify any point size, use variable leading and letter spacing, and even justify paragraphs! The result is a nearly WYSIWYG match between what you see on-screen in WebPlus and what ends up in the Web browser. Because HTML positions elements using absolute co-ordinates, overlapping elements are allowed, and file sizes are reduced.

In theory, you can use any font you like. However, if a specified font isn't present on a visitor's computer, an available font will be substituted, with unpredictable results for your beautifully designed layout! As a rule, stick with the WebSafe fonts available within WebPlus, i.e. Times New Roman, Arial, Tahoma, Verdana. They are denoted in the fonts list with a green tick and all other fonts have a blue question mark.

The WebPlus Layout Checker Wizard will warn you if your site uses non-standard fonts or character properties, text that must be output as a graphic, or other problems.

Startup Wizard

Once WebPlus has been installed, you'll be ready to start. Setup adds a **Serif WebPlus 10** item to the **(All) Programs** submenu of the Windows **Start** menu.

- Use the Windows **Start** button to start WebPlus (or if WebPlus is already running, choose **New** from the File menu) to display the Startup Wizard (menu screen).

Startup Wizard

The Startup Wizard presents several choices:

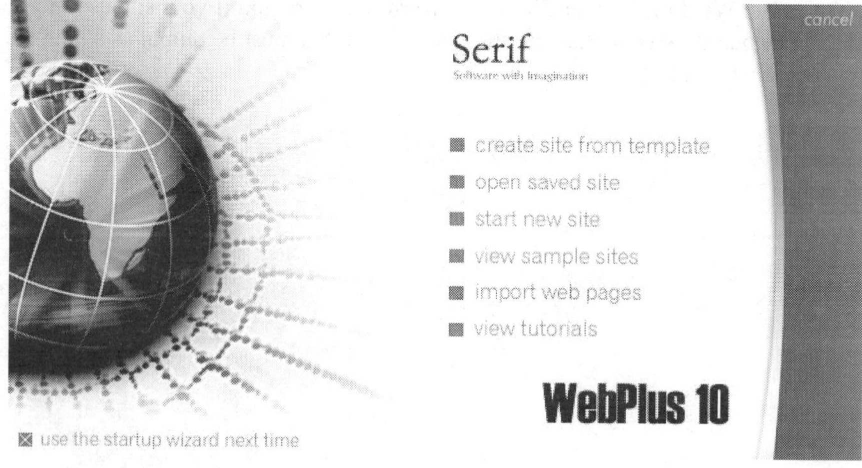

The choices are summarized as follows:

- **create site from template**, to create an instant Web site
- **open saved site**, to edit existing WebPlus project files
- **start new site**, to start out with a blank Home page
- **view sample sites**, to see professionally designed examples
- **import web pages**, to convert existing HTML resources
- **view tutorials**, to see introductory illustrated overviews

To get started, click **start new site**.

The Startup Wizard is displayed by default when you launch WebPlus. You can switch it off (or back on) via the **Use the startup wizard next time** check box on the Startup Wizard screen, or via the **Use Startup Wizard** option on the General tab of **Tools>Options...**.

Creating a Web site using a template

The first time you launch WebPlus, you'll see the **Startup Wizard**, with a menu of six choices. The first of these is **Create Site from Template**. Using a template speeds you through the process of creating a professional site. Whether you're just beginning to work with WebPlus—or an old hand exploring new design possibilities—put WebPlus templates to work for you!

To create a Web site using a template:

1. Launch WebPlus, or choose **Startup Wizard...** from the File menu, to display the Startup Wizard.
2. Click **Create Site from Template**, select a site category on the left, and examine the samples on the right. Click the sample that's closest to what you want, then click **Finish**.

The site opens to the first (Home) page, with the Studio's Site tab displayed on the right, showing the various pages that comprise the site in its Site Structure tree.

Opening an existing Web site

You can open an existing WebPlus site from the Startup Wizard, via the File menu or Standard toolbar. A range of other file formats, including WebPlus templates and Serif PagePlus files can also be opened.

It is also possible to use the Startup Wizard option, **Import Web Pages**, to **import pages** from existing HTML Web sites.

To open an existing WebPlus site (Startup Wizard):

1. Select the **Open Saved Site** option. In the Documents pane of the **Open Saved Work** dialog, you'll see either your computer's folder structure for navigation to your web sites (Folders tab) or a list of most recently used web sites (History tab). Preview thumbnails or web site details can be shown in the adjacent pane depending on your current view.
2. Click a file name or sample, then click **Open**. The site opens to the first (Home) page.

To open an existing WebPlus site (during WebPlus session):

1. Choose **Open...** from the File menu.
   OR
   Click the **Open** button on the Standard toolbar.
2. In the Open dialog, select the folder and file name and click the **Open** button.

To revert to the saved version of an open site:

- Choose **Revert...** from the File menu.

Open dialog options

The Open dialog has two options for intermediate to advanced users.

In the **Files of type** list, you can select WebPlus Site (*.WPP), **WebPlus templates** (*.WPX) files, and PagePlus documents (*.PPP; up to version 9).

Check the **Open as Untitled** box if you want a saved file to open as Untitled—for example, if you're about to create a new site from an old one and want to leave the old one intact. This is the default option for template files.

Importing HTML Web pages and sites

The **Import Web Pages** option lets you import one or more HTML or XHTML pages into your new or existing WebPlus site, with control over which additional elements are imported.

To import one or more HTML Web pages:

1. (From the Startup Wizard) Select the **Import Web Pages** option.
   OR
   (From the WebPlus workspace) Choose **Import Web Pages...** from the File menu.
2. In the dialog, select whether to import a **Single page** or a **Site (multiple pages)** and type or click **Browse...** to designate either a Web Address (a URL from a live web site) or a local HTML/XHTML file(s).
3. When importing more than one page, specify the **Followed hyperlink depth**—how many links "away" from the starting page WebPlus should proceed when importing. For example, a depth of 1 would mean "one link away": WebPlus would follow each link on the starting page and import each secondary page. With a depth setting of 2, WebPlus would repeat the link-following from each secondary page, and so on.
4. Designate a **Preferred page width** for the imported pages.

5. Clicking the **Advanced>>** button lets you select which types of file (**Images**, **Text**, **Sound files**, **Video files**, **Java applets**, **Meta data**, **Server sided script**, **JavaScript**, **hotspots** or **forms**) WebPlus should import.
6. Click **Import...** to proceed with importing. Click **Close** to dismiss the dialog.

The imported page(s) appear in the Site tab's Site Structure tree.

Starting a Web site from scratch

Although **Web Templates** can simplify your design choices, you can just as easily start out from scratch with a new, blank web site.

To start a new site from scratch using the Startup Wizard:

- Launch WebPlus, and click **Start New Site**.

The new site opens with a blank page using default **page properties**.

If you click **Cancel** (or press **Escape**) from the Startup Wizard, you'll get the same result.

To start a new site during your WebPlus session:

- Choose **New** from the File menu.

The Startup Wizard is displayed by default when you launch WebPlus. You can switch it off (or back on) via the **Use the startup wizard next time** check box on the Startup Wizard screen, or via the **Use Startup Wizard** option on the General tab of **Tools>Options...**.

Working with more than one site

WebPlus lets you open more than one site at a time. Each new site you open appears in a separate window with its own settings. Convenient tabs let you switch quickly between windows, and with windows reduced or tiled you can drag and drop objects between windows. You can also preview the current site in a separate window (see **Previewing your Web site** on p. 209).

To specify the placement of window tabs:

- Choose **Window Tabs** from the View menu and select **None**, **Top**, or **Bottom**.

None hides the tabs; **Top** or **Bottom** show them either above or below the workspace.

To close the current window:

- Choose **Close** from the File menu or click the window's **Close** button at the upper right. If it's the only window open for the site, the command closes the project and you'll be prompted to save changes.

You can close all open sites without exiting the main WebPlus application.

The **Window** menu lets you arrange the currently open windows, i.e. by cascading, or tiling horizontally or vertically.

The **Window** menu also lists the names of open site windows, with the current window checked. The easiest way to switch between windows, of course, is simply to click the tab for the window you want (or click directly in the window). However, if one window is obscuring another, press **Ctrl+Tab** or click a window's name on the menu to switch to another window.

Saving your WebPlus project

To save your work:

- Click the **Save** button on the Standard toolbar (or **Ctrl+S**).
OR

- To save under a different name, choose **Save As...** from the File menu.

Using templates

If you've created a document layout that you think would make a good basis for future Web pages, you can save the layout as a **template** (*.WPX) file. When opening a saved template file, WebPlus automatically opens an untitled copy, leaving the original template intact. Templates help ensure continuity between your documents by preserving starting setups for such elements as headlines, body text, and graphics.

To save a site as a template:

- Choose **Save As...** from the File menu. Under "Save as type," click to select the **WebPlus Template (*.wpx)** option. Enter a file name, leaving the .WPX extension intact, and click **Save**.

To open a template file:

1. Choose **Open...** from the File menu and select **WebPlus Templates (*.wpx)** in the "Files of type" box.

2. If you want to open the original template file, uncheck the **Open as Untitled** option. To open an untitled copy, leave the box checked.

3. Click the **Open** button.

Closing WebPlus

To close the current window:

- Choose **Close** from the File menu or click the window's **Close** button. If it's the only window open for the site, the command closes the project and you'll be prompted to save changes.

You can close all open windows without exiting the main WebPlus application.

To close all open windows:

- Choose **Close All** from the file menu.

To close WebPlus:

- Choose **Exit** from the File menu.

You'll be prompted to save changes to any open projects.

Developing Sites and Pages

3

Understanding site structure and navigation

Unlike a printed publication, a Web site doesn't depend on a linear page sequence. When designing a site, it makes more sense to think of the site in spatial terms, with a **structure** like that of a museum which people will explore. You can generally assume that your visitors will come in through the "front door" (the **Home page**)—but where they go after that depends on the links you've provided. These **navigation** pathways are like corridors that connect the various rooms of the museum. It's up to you as the "architect" to develop a sensible arrangement of pages and links so that visitors can find their way around easily, without getting lost.

In WebPlus, you can use the **Site Structure tree** to visually map out the structure of your site and then add **navigation elements**—special **theme graphics** that dynamically adapt to the structure you've defined. You'll encounter the Site Structure tree frequently as you learn about working with pages.

Site structure

Unlike the museum in our analogy, the "structure" of a Web site has nothing to do with its physical layout, or where pages are stored. Rather, it's a way of logically arranging the content on the site so that visitors have an easier time navigating through it. One of the most useful organizing principles—which WebPlus strongly reinforces—is an "inverted tree" structure which can branch out to other pages. To the visitor navigating your site, this arrangement presents your content in a familiar, hierarchical way, structured into **sections** and **levels**.

A **section** is a content category, for example "Who's Who?," "Products," or "Links." The various major sections are typically listed on the site's Home page in a navigation bar. Ideally, each page on the site belongs to a particular section. And unless there's only one page in a given section, the section will have its own main page, which usually serves as a menu for subsidiary pages.

The **level** is the number of steps (i.e. jumps) a given page is removed from the Home page. The Home page will always reside at Level 1, normally along with main section menu pages. This allows navigation bars to work easily and automatically. Pages one step "below" the section menu pages reside at Level 2, and so on.

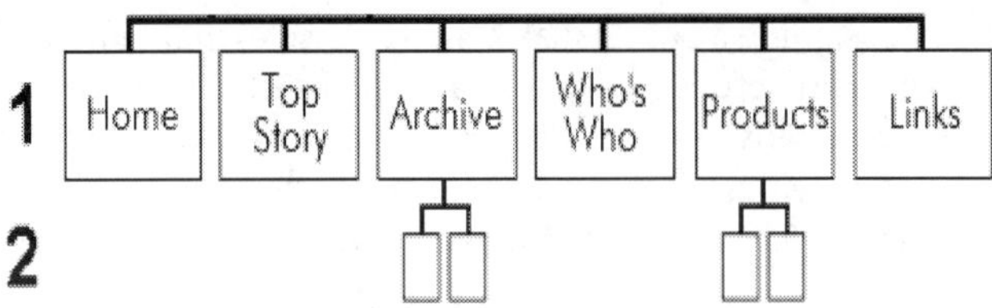

In WebPlus, the Site Structure tree (in the **Site tab**) provides a visual aid that lets you organize the content on your site into sections and levels—in other words as a hierarchy of **parent** pages branching to **child** pages. Here's how a similar structure might appear in the WebPlus Site Structure tree:

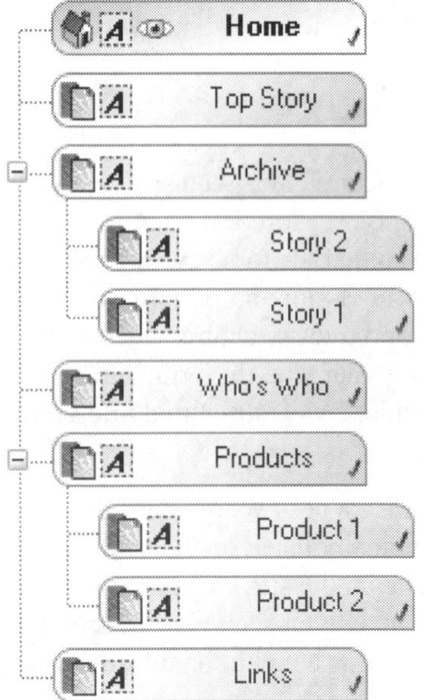

The Site Structure tree makes it easy to visualize relationships between pages and lay out your site in a way that makes sense for the content you have to offer. Of course, a Web site is truly an interconnected web of pages, and the tree structure doesn't prevent you from installing links between any two pages. But it does expose the major pathways within your site—up, down, and sideways. Logical section/level design makes your site easier to navigate, and WebPlus makes it simple to create **navigation bars** that mirror your site structure and help guide your visitors along those "main roads."

Navigation

In WebPlus, certain types of **theme graphic** we'll call "navigation elements"—such as Previous/Next buttons and Navigation bars (or "navbars" for short) are pre-programmed to understand your site structure, making it easy to design a site that's simple to navigate. You simply select one from the Studio's Theme Graphics tab and WebPlus does the rest! Previous/Next buttons automatically link laterally, to adjacent pages on the same level. Navbars combine buttons with popup menus to facilitate movement between the various sections and levels of a site.

For example, here's a navbar we selected for the site shown in the tree on the previous page. The buttons provide links to the Home and section menu pages (all at Level 1) and popup menus that link to child pages (Level 2 in this case).

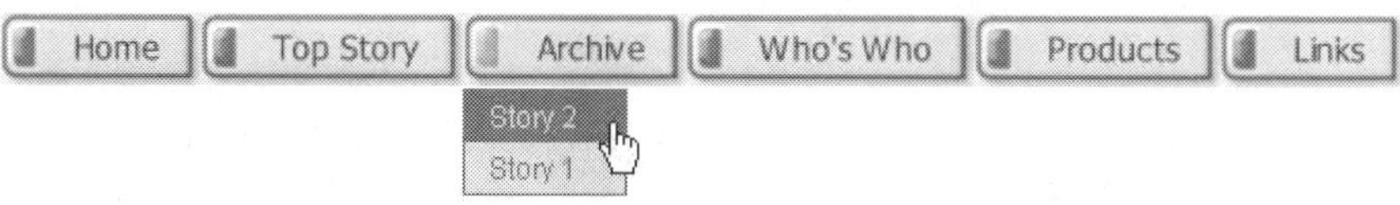

Here's a brief summary of the advantages of incorporating navigation elements in your site design:

- You can install navigation elements at any level of your site, and (for navbars) easily customize which part(s) of the site structure each navbar should link to—for example, to top-level pages, pages on the same level, child pages, etc.
- Because navigation elements are theme graphics, you can use the Theme Graphics tab to select co-ordinated design elements (buttons, etc.) for a consistent look, and change the overall appearance with a single click.
- By default, all pages in the tree are "included in navigation"—that is, they can be linked to by navigation elements. You can **exclude** certain pages so they'll be ignored by navigation elements. Included pages show a ✓ mark in their page entry, while an excluded page lacks the mark. For example, suppose you had a section of reference pages that you didn't want visitors to explore top-down. Excluding the parent page for that section would remove it from the navbar. Of course, you can still create hyperlinks to the page—it just won't appear in navigation elements.

- Best of all, a WebPlus navigation element updates dynamically if you subsequently alter page names or relationships, or cut/paste the navbar to another page. For example, "Story 1" above is just a placeholder for an actual title—common practice when designing a site before all the intended content is in place. Once we have the actual story, suppose we rename that page to "Smith Appointed to Board of Directors"... the navbar would instantly reflect the change!

Understanding pages and master pages

Pages are the basic unit of Web design. WebPlus lets you structure your site's content by arranging pages into a branching "tree," which in turn helps visitors navigate through the site. Looking at individual pages from a design standpoint, each WebPlus page has a "foreground" **page layer** and a "background" **master page layer**.

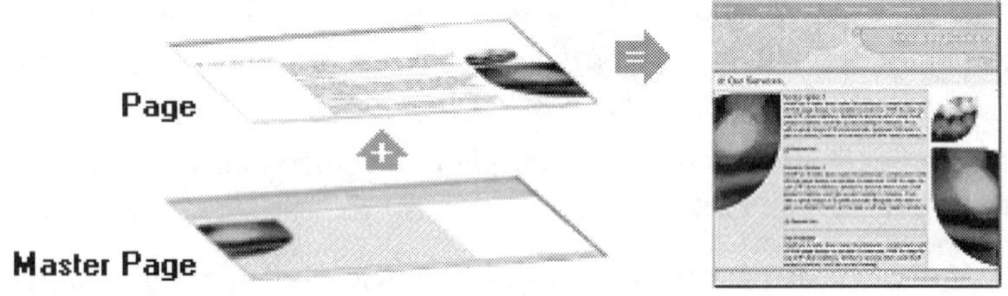

Master pages are part of the structure of your WebPlus project, and provide a flexible way to store background elements that you would like to appear on more than one page—for example a logo, background, border design, or even a navigation element. The key concept here is that a particular master page is typically shared by multiple pages, as illustrated below. By placing a design element on a master page and then assigning several pages to use that master page, you ensure that all the pages incorporate that element. Of course, each individual page can have its own elements.

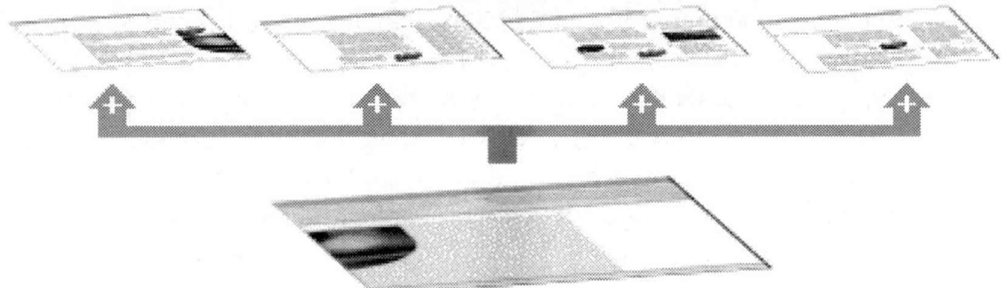

The Studio's **Site** tab includes an upper Master Pages section with icons for each master page, and a Site Structure section that provides feedback indicating which master page is being used by not only the currently viewed page, but also other pages in the site:

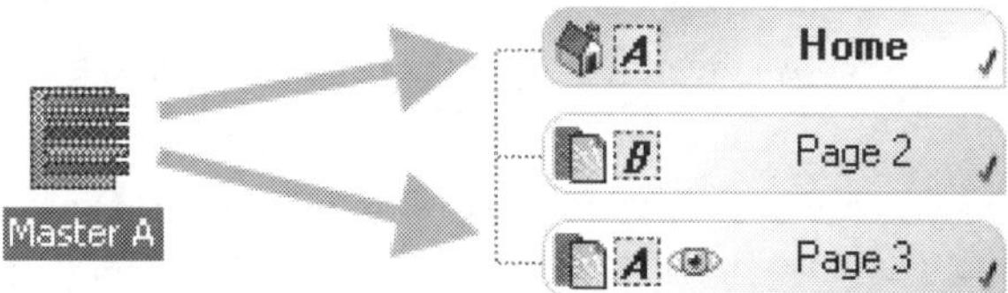

Viewing Pages

The WebPlus workspace consists of a "page" area and a surrounding "pasteboard" area.

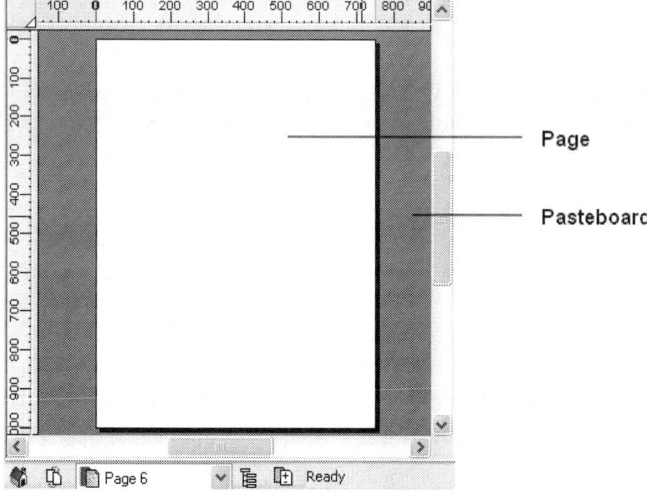

The **page** area is where you put the text, graphics, and other elements that you want to appear on your final Web page. The **pasteboard** is where you generally keep elements that are being prepared or waiting to be positioned on the page area. When you publish your Web site from the WebPlus project, anything which overlaps the page area appears, while anything entirely on the pasteboard does not. The pasteboard is shared by all pages and master pages, and it's useful for copying or moving objects between pages.

To move or copy an object between pages via the pasteboard:

1. Drag the object from the source page onto the pasteboard (hold down the **Ctrl** key to copy).
2. Display the target page (see "Switching between pages" below).
3. Drag (or **Ctrl**-drag to copy) the object from the pasteboard onto the target page.

WebPlus makes it easy to see exactly what you're working on—from a wide view of a whole page to a close-up view of a small region. For example, you can use the **scroll bars** at the right and bottom of the main window to move the page and pasteboard with respect to the main window. The view automatically re-centres itself as you drag objects to the edge of the screen.

The **View toolbar** at the top of the screen provides the **Pan Tool** as an alternative way of moving around, plus a number of buttons that let you **zoom in** and **out** so you can inspect and/or edit the page at different levels of detail.

Hint: If you're using a wheel mouse, spinning the wheel scrolls vertically. **Shift**-spin to scroll horizontally and **Ctrl**-spin to zoom in or out!

Switching between pages

WebPlus provides a variety of ways of getting quickly to the part of your site you need to work on. The Studio's Site tab provides a central "control panel" including both the **Site Structure tree**, which depicts the hierarchy of pages in your site (see **Understanding site structure and navigation** on p. 31), and icons for each of the site's **master pages**. The Site tab lets you switch between pages, and view or set **page properties**.

The Site Structure dialog (click the **Site Structure** button) affords similar tree-based functionality, and the HintLine's **Page Locator** offers yet another convenient method of jumping to a particular page.

Selecting vs. viewing a page: Single-clicking a page/master page entry merely **selects** the page, which you might do for example if you were about to delete it by right-clicking. To actually **view** the associated page/master page you need to double-click an entry or use one of the methods noted below. Feedback from the entry tells you whether it's currently viewed and/or selected, i.e.

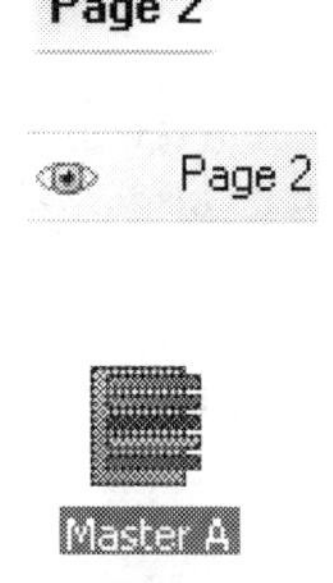

A dark turquoise entry (with bolded page name) denotes the selected page.

The eye icon denotes the currently viewed page—which you're able to edit in the workspace. This example shows a viewed (but unselected) page.

A highlighted master page icon in the Site tab's upper window denotes the selected master page.

Master A

An eye icon in the master page icon (Site tab's upper window) denotes the currently viewed page—which you're able to edit in the workspace. This example shows a viewed (but unselected) master page.

To view a specific page/master page:

Several methods can be used to view a page:

- On the Studio's **Site** tab, double-click the entry for the page (or master page) you want to view. The Site Structure window of the tab includes a tree with entries for pages in the site, while the Master Pages window shows only master pages as thumbnails. You may need to click the **Master Pages** button to display the master pages window.

- On the HintLine, click the entry for the page or master page in the **Page Locator** list.

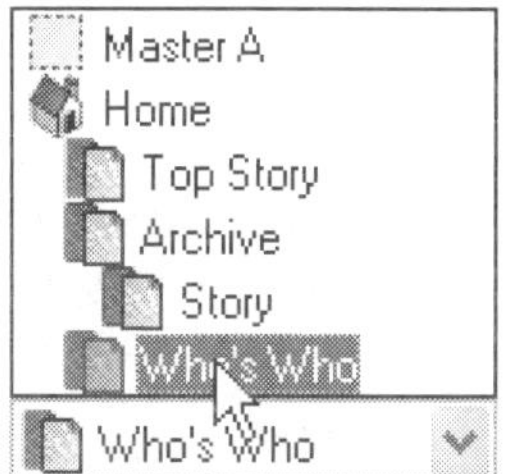

- Click the **Site Structure** button on the HintLine or on the Site tab's Page window. Select the page entry in the dialog's tree (double-click tree entries if necessary to expand each branch). Then click the **View Page** button.

For master pages:

- On the Studio's **Site** tab, click the Master Pages ▶ button to reveal a master page window. One or more master page icons will be displayed.
- Double-click the icon for the master page you want to view.

To switch between the master page and page layer (for the current page):

- Click the **Page/Master Page** button on the HintLine.
  OR
- Choose **Master Page** from the View menu (or **Page** to switch back).

As a shortcut to view the site's Home page:

- Click the Home Page button on the HintLine.

Adding, removing, and rearranging pages

Using the Studio's **Site** tab, you can quickly add or delete pages at any level of your site structure, and use drag-and-drop to rearrange pages within the structure as needed, add new master pages, reassign pages to particular master pages, and add offsite links. Use the upper Master Pages window of the Site tab to access master pages, and the Pages window (tab's central Site Structure tree) to access pages. Besides the Site tab, WebPlus offers a variety of other ways to manipulate pages: the **Site Structure** dialog, the **Master Page Manager**, and both standard and right-click (context) menus.

To add a new page at a particular level:

1. In the Pages Window (Site Structure tree) of the Studio's Site tab, select a page after which you want to add the new page. A single click on the page's entry suffices to select the page (its page name will become bold); double-clicking also displays the page in the workspace.
2. To add one page after the original page, click the **Add** button directly above the Pages window.

A new page appears at the same level as the original page, following it and using the same master page. As described below, you can always move the page to a different position or level, or switch to a different master page.

If you wish, you can use a dialog to insert a new page at any point in the site structure, with the option of copying design elements from an original page, and using any master page.

To add a new page anywhere:

1. Choose **Page...** from the Insert menu.
   OR
   Right-click any page entry in the Site tab's Site Structure tree and choose **Insert Page...**.
   OR
   Click the **Site Structure** button just above the Site Structure tree (or on the HintLine), or choose Site Structure... from the File menu. In the Site Structure dialog, click the **Insert Page...** button.
2. In the dialog, specify options for the new page:
   • Type an optional page name. (If you don't type a name, WebPlus will apply a default name.)
   • Specify which master page the new page should use.
   • To duplicate the design elements from a particular page, check **Copy objects from page** and select the source page in the activated list.
   • In the Placement section, specify the page in the site structure from which you can insert a page Before, After, or make it a Child of the named page.
3. Click **OK**.

A new page appears at the specified location in the site structure.

You can also add an **offsite link** to your site structure. Typically, this would be a page separate from your site that you wanted to include in your site's navigation structure (for example, in a popup menu). The offsite link appears in the Site Structure tree and in navigation elements, so you can manipulate it just as if it were a page in your site.

To add an offsite link:

1. Right-click any page entry in the Site tab's Site Structure tree and choose **Insert Offsite Link...**.
2. In the dialog, click to select the link destination type, and enter the specific offsite hyperlink target (see **Adding hyperlinks and anchors** on p. 149), and the window (**Same Window** or **New Window**) in which you want the target to appear.
3. Type a Menu name to identify the offsite link in the Site Structure tree (the equivalent of its page name).
4. Click **OK**.

To add a new master page:

- On the Studio's Site tab, ensure the 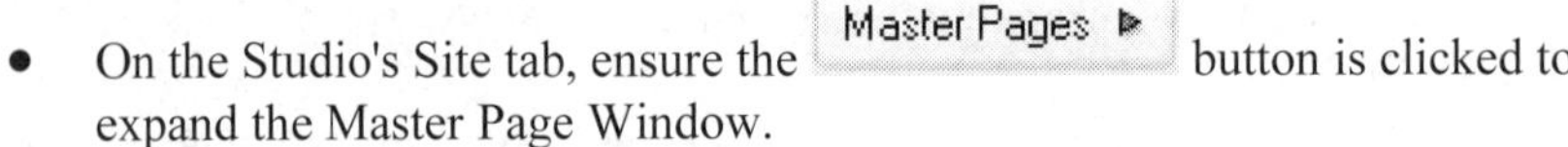 button is clicked to expand the Master Page Window.

- Click the **Add** button above the Master Pages window.
  OR

1. Click the **Master Page Manager** button above the Master Pages window (or on the HintLine), or choose the item from the View menu.
2. Select the dialog's Add tab. Enter Width and/or Height settings if different from the defaults.
3. (Optional) From the Background tab, set a background page colour (or use a picture).
4. (Optional) From the Page Transitions tab, select an entry and/or exit transition (after checking Override master page setting) when navigating between pages using the master page.
5. Click **OK**.

A new master page appears.

To delete a page or master page:

1. On the Studio's Site tab, select the page (or master page) to delete by clicking its entry.
2. Click the **.Remove** button above the appropriate window to delete the page.

When you delete a page, you'll have the option to **remove** any hyperlinks in your site that point to it, or **redirect** the hyperlinks to another specified page.

Rearranging pages

Besides using the Site Structure tree to add or delete pages, you can use it to rearrange pages as needed. As explained in **Understanding site structure and navigation** on p. 31, the tree provides a visual aid that lets you organize the content on your site into "sections" and "levels"—that is, as a hierarchy of **parent** pages branching to **child** pages. Not only does the tree help you keep track of your content, but WebPlus translates your logical page arrangement into a site that's easy to navigate. Special theme graphics called navigation elements like Previous/Next buttons and navigation bars (navbars) are pre-programmed to understand your site structure and will update dynamically if you rearrange pages!

Using the parent/child structure, rearranging pages is an intuitive process whether you use drag-and-drop or convenient buttons. You can move a page:

- To a different sequential position (up or down) at the same level of the structure
- To a higher (parent) level
- To a lower (child) level

To move a page:

1. Display the Studio's Site tab or the Site Structure dialog.
2. Single-click to select the page in the Site Structure tree. (On the Site tab, a single click on the page's entry suffices to select the page; double-clicking also displays the page in the workspace.)
3. (Using drag-and-drop) Drag the page entry up or down and drop it at a new position in the tree. Watch the cursor for feedback on the new position relative to that of the page just below the cursor:

   or moves the page to the same level as, and following, the page below the cursor;

   or makes the page a child of the page below the cursor.

   OR

(Using buttons) Click one of the buttons adjacent to the Site Structure tree. The button names convey the resulting actions:

Move Page Down At Same Level

Move Page Up At Same Level

Make Page a Child

Make Page a Parent

Assigning master pages

If you've defined more than one master page for your site, you can use a variety of methods to reassign a specific master page to individual pages, one page at a time. You can also set a page to use no master page—for example, if you import an HTML page you may want to see only its original design elements without adding others from a master page. The key thing to remember is that each page can use only one master page. (For an overview, see Understanding pages and master pages.)

To assign a master page to a page:

- On the Studio's **Site** tab, click on the master page thumbnail (in the Master Pages section) and drag onto the page entry (in the Site Structure section).
  OR

1. Click the **Master Page Manager** button above the Master Pages window (or on the HintLine), or choose the item from the View menu.
2. In the dialog's Set Page Masters box, select a page name in the **Site page(s)** drop-down menu. Then select a different master page in the **Uses master page** drop-down menu, or select "(none)" to assign no master page. Click **OK**.

Working in frames

WebPlus allows one or more frames, also known as **Iframes**, to be place on a single page, each accessing another page within of your web site. Just like an image, a frame can be placed anywhere on the page and can be drawn to any size. While it's typical to link to a page it's possible to link to a range of other link destinations (an Internet page, local file or stored user data) as well.

A great way of always showing the same page (e.g. showing a product list) within every page in your site is to apply a frame to the site's master page. Taking the idea further, you can add selection buttons (or menu options) in support of the frame to change what the frame displays (according to the currently selected option).

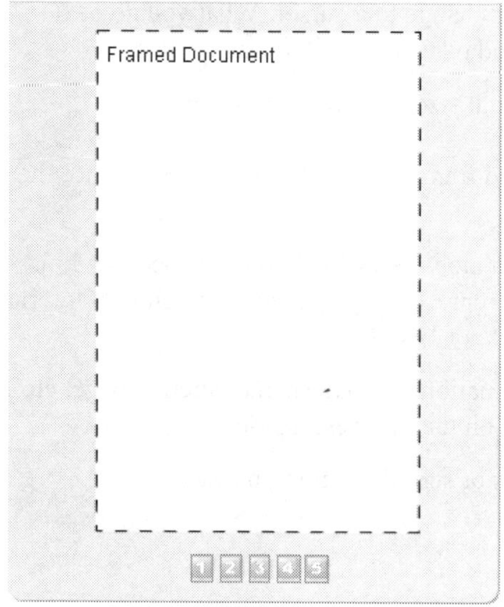

If each button links to a different page (but always to the same frame) you can make your framed documents contents change with button contents—this takes advantage of the automatically generated **HTML ID** (see p. 171) which should be referenced as the Target Frame name in each button's hyperlink.

If adding a frame to a master page remember to ensure that frame's destination page is independent and not based on the same master page.

Frames are applied via the **Framed Document Tool**. The term "Framed Document" is used in WebPlus to keep the concept of Iframes distinct from that of HTML or Creative text frames (used for controlling the placement of text on the page)—both very different features within WebPlus.

Frames are fully supported in all the latest Internet browsers.

To create a framed document:

1. Select the page on which you would like to add a frame.
2. From the Web Objects toolbar, select the **Framed Document Tool**. You'll see the mouse pointer change to a cursor. What you do next determines the initial size and placement of the frame.
3. To insert the frame at a default size, simply click the mouse.
   OR
   To set the size of the inserted frame, drag out a region and release the mouse button.
4. A dialog is displayed immediately into which you can specify a link destination. Choose an icon representing a page in your site, an Internet page, a file on your hard disk, or User Data.
5. Set the frame contents information (the page name, internet page, etc.) which will differ depending on the link destination.
6. Optionally choose if borders or scrollbars are to be used.
7. Click **OK**.

Using layout aids

WebPlus provides a variety of layout aids to assist you in placing design elements accurately: layout guides, page margin settings, and rulers. When the snapping feature is turned on, objects you create, move, or resize will jump to align with nearby, visible layout guides and ruler guides.

Layout guides are visual guide lines that help you position layout elements, either "by eye" or with snapping (see below) turned on.

Page margin settings are fundamental to your layout, and usually are among the first choices you'll make after starting a site from scratch. Narrow margins around the perimeter are a good starting point for clean page design. The page margins are shown as a blue box which is actually four guide lines—for top, bottom, left, and right—indicating the underlying page margin settings. If you like, you can set the margins to match your current printer settings.

You also have the option of setting up **row** and **column guides** as an underlying layout aid. WebPlus represents rows and columns on the page area with dashed blue guide lines.

In addition, you can define free-floating **ruler guides** on a page by clicking on the WebPlus rulers.

Unlike **frame margins and columns**, these layout guides don't control where frame text flows. Rather, they serve as visual aids that help you match your frame layout to the desired column layout. Usually the frame column width matches the underlying page column guides, but sometimes (for example in multiple-column layouts) the frame column will take up two, or even three, of the page columns.

To define layout guides:

- Choose **Layout Guides...** from the Edit menu.
  OR

- Right-click on a blank part of the page and choose **Layout Guides...**.

The **Margins** tab lets you set guide lines for page margins, rows, and columns. You can set the left, right, top, and bottom margins individually. The dialog also provides options for **balanced margins** (left matching right, top matching bottom).

Use the **Row and Column Guides** section to define guides for rows and columns. If you want rows or columns of uneven width, first place them at fixed intervals, then later drag on the guides to reposition them as required.

To show or hide layout guides you've defined:

- Check or uncheck **Guide Lines** on the View menu.

This setting also affects any ruler guides you've placed on the page area.

Rulers

The WebPlus **rulers** mimic the paste-up artist's T-square, and serve several purposes:

- To act as a measuring tool
- To create ruler guides for aligning and snapping
- To define the dot grid, and (indirectly) the snapping grid

To select the measurement interval:

- Choose **Options...** from the Tools menu and select the **Rulers** page.

Units are expressed in pixels only and can be set for horizontal and vertical rulers.

The actual interval size of the ruler marks depends on the current zoom percentage. In zoomed-out view, for example at 50%, there's more distance between ruler marks than when zoomed-in to 150%. To handle work where you want finer control or smaller snapping increments, click a zoom button to magnify the page.

By default, the horizontal ruler lies along the top of the WebPlus window and the vertical ruler along the left edge. The default **ruler intersection** is the top left corner of the pasteboard area. The default **zero point** (marked as 0 on each ruler) is the top-left corner of the page area.

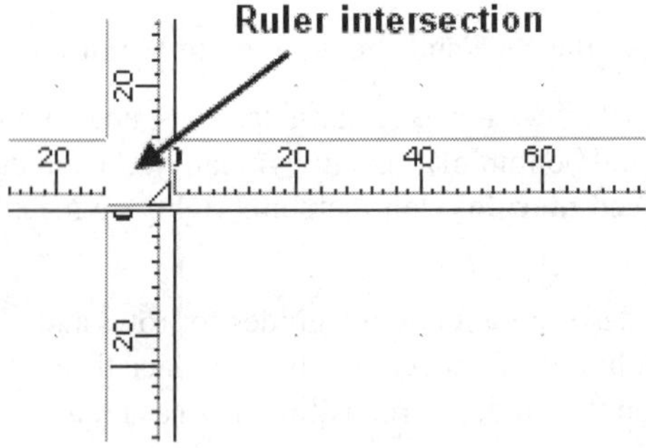

To define a new zero point:

- Click and drag the arrow on the ruler intersection to the new zero point on the page or pasteboard.

To move the rulers:

- With the **Shift** key down, click and drag the arrow on the ruler intersection. The zero point remains unchanged.

- Double-click on the ruler intersection to make the rulers and zero point jump to the top left-hand corner of the currently selected object. This comes in handy for measuring page objects.

To restore the original ruler position and zero point:

- Double-click the arrow on the ruler intersection.

To lock the rulers and prevent them from being moved:

- Choose **Tools>Options...** and select the **Rulers** page, then check **Lock Rulers**.

If the ruler intersection is greyed, the rulers are currently locked.

Rulers as a measuring tool

The most obvious role for rulers is as a measuring tool. As you move the mouse pointer, small lines along each ruler display the current horizontal and vertical cursor position. When you click to select an object, white ruler regions indicate the object's left, right, top, and bottom edges. Each region has a zero point relative to the object's upper left corner, so you can see the object's dimensions at a glance.

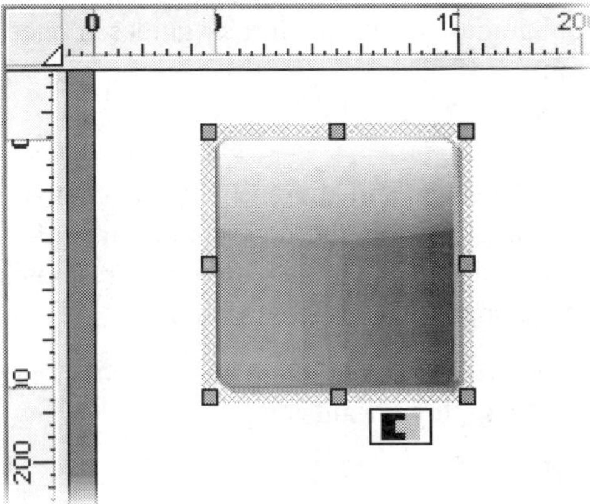

Creating ruler guides

WebPlus lets you to set up horizontal and vertical **ruler guides**—non-printing, red lines you can use to align headlines, pictures, and other layout elements.

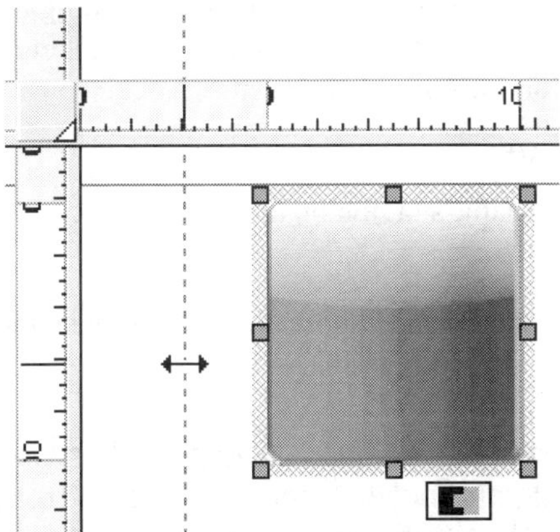

- To create a ruler guide, click on a ruler and drag onto the workspace. The red dashed ruler guide line appears, changing to a solid line when the mouse button is released.

- To move a guide, drag it (the double arrow cursor shows; see example).
- To remove a guide, drag and drop it anywhere outside the page area.
- To lock ruler guides, choose **Tools>Options...** and select the **Rulers** page, then check **Lock Ruler Guides**.
- To fine-position ruler guides, choose **Layout Guides...** from the Edit menu (or right-click menu) and select the **Guides** tab. You can use the tab to create or delete individual guides. To delete all ruler guides at once, click the **Remove All** button.

Snapping

The **Snapping** feature simplifies placement and alignment by "magnetizing" grid dots and guide lines. When snapping is on, the edges and centres of objects you create, move, or resize will jump to align with the nearest visible grid dot or guide. Objects normally snap to the page edge, too.

Guide lines include ruler guides as well as layout guide lines based on page margins, rows, and columns (see **Using layout aids** on p. 44).

To turn snapping on and off:

- Click the **Snapping** button on the HintLine toolbar. When the button is down, snapping is on.

Selective snapping

You control which points and lines are snapped to by showing or hiding the individual guide elements (i.e., Rulers, Guide lines, Frames, Dot Grid, etc.), and by changing options settings for those visible elements.

To show or hide guide elements:

- Enable (or disable) the element name's button on the View menu.
  OR
- Right-click on the page or pasteboard and choose View, then select the element's name.

The "Guide Lines" setting controls ruler guides you've placed as well as page margin guides and row/column guides. "Frames" controls frame borders, margins, and columns. "Dot Grid" controls the dot grid.

To set which visible elements are snapped to:

1. Choose **Options...** from the Tools menu, and select the Layout option.
2. Check the "Snap to:" box, then check/uncheck the elements you want to snap to. The choices include **Grid dots**, **Page/Bleed edge**, **Page margins**, **Ruler guides**, **Row/column guides** and **Nearest Pixel**.

Using the dot grid

The dot grid is a matrix of dots or lines based on ruler units, covering the page and pasteboard areas. Like ruler guides, it's handy for both visual alignment and snapping.

To turn the dot grid on and off:

- Enable (or disable) the **Dot Grid** button on the View menu.
  OR
- Choose **Options...** from the Tools menu and select **Layout**. Check or uncheck **Dot Grid**.

You can set the grid spacing, style, and colour via the Options dialog.

To change the grid spacing, style, and/or colour:

1. To set the grid interval, enter a value (in pixels) in the **Grid lines** box.
2. To display the grid using dots, select "Dots" in the **Grid** option. To display grid lines or crosses, select "Solid" or "Crosses", respectively.
3. To change the colour of grid dots, click the **Colour** button and then select a colour thumbnail. Use **More Colours..** to access the Colour Selector dialog.

Incorporating theme graphics

The Studio's **Theme Graphics tab** provides a wide selection of ready-made themed objects, which you can add to your pages with a single click. (Or you can use a dialog if you prefer.) Theme graphics range from static "design elements" like bullets to hyperlinked **"navigation elements"** like Previous/Next buttons and navigation bars pre-programmed to adapt to the **site structure** you've defined. Theme graphics behave as single objects, with built-in responses to being resized, rolled over with the mouse on a Web page, and so on. Where applicable, you can edit the text or other properties of a theme graphic once it's been added to a page. Once you've added theme graphics to your site, you can instantly update any or all of them to use a different theme.

Using the Theme Graphics tab, you can view and select theme graphics in two ways: by **type** or by **set**. A "type" is a particular category of design element—for example, bullets and buttons are two different types. A "set" is a collection of elements using the same visual theme, with one element of each type and a descriptive name for the visual theme—such as Bright, Candy, Clean, etc. For example:

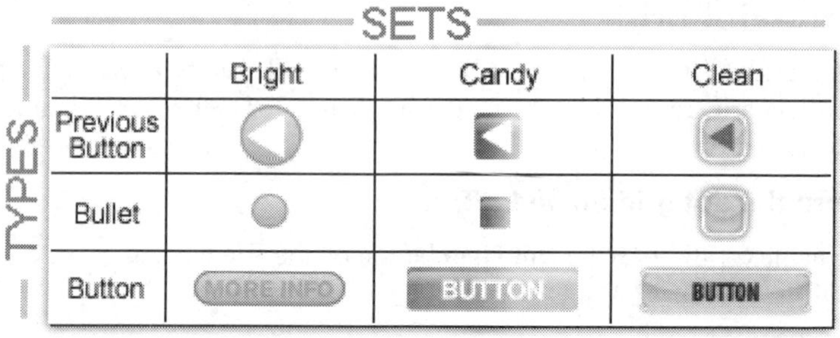

SETS

TYPES

	Bright	Candy	Clean
Previous Button			
Bullet			
Button	MORE INFO	BUTTON	BUTTON

For a consistent appearance throughout your site, choose theme graphics from a single set. Then if you decide to go for a different "look" later on, simply click a different set on the Theme Graphics tab to instantly update all your theme graphics, as explained below.

To add a theme graphic to a page:

1. Display the Studio's **Theme Graphics** tab.
2. In the Categories tree, select a category to browse.
   Click **Current Site** to view theme graphics already in use, for example if you want to add an element again.
   OR
   Expand the **Sets** or **Types** list, and then select a category to view its gallery.
   OR
   With "Theme Graphics" selected as a category, click the **Current Site**, **View Sets**, or **View Types** thumbnail in the lower Theme Graphics section. Then click the thumbnail for the type or set you want to browse.
3. Browse the gallery of available elements and click a particular theme graphic to add it at the centre of your page. You can also drag from the gallery thumbnail and drop an element at a specific location.
   OR
4. Click the 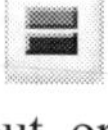 **Insert Theme Graphic** button on the Tools toolbar's Insert flyout, or choose **Theme Graphic...** from the Insert menu.

5. Select a theme **type** from the list at the top of the dialog, and choose a theme **set** by clicking a thumbnail in the lower gallery.

6. Click **OK**.

In the Theme Graphics gallery, clicking a thumbnail triggers the default action. You can right-click the thumbnail or click its down arrow to view a popup menu with other actions Insert, Replace in Selection, or Replace in Site.

Once you've added theme graphics to your site, you can instantly update any or all of them to use a different theme.

To update theme graphics to use a different theme:

1. Display the Studio's **Theme Graphics** tab.

2. Expand the **Sets** list in the Categories tree, then select the theme you want to apply.
   OR
   With "Theme Graphics" selected as a category, click the **View Sets** thumbnail in the lower Theme Graphics section. Then click the thumbnail for the theme you want to apply.

3. You can perform several functions:

   - To update a **specific theme graphic**: Select it and note its type on the HintLine, then right-click the thumbnail of the *same element type* in the gallery. Choose **Replace in Selection** from the popup menu.

   - To update **all elements** of a particular type: Select a representative theme graphic of that type, then right-click the thumbnail of the *same element type* in the gallery. Choose **Replace All** from the popup menu.

   - To update **all theme graphics in your site**: Click the **Apply <Theme>** thumbnail in the lower Theme Graphics section (see note below). This action updates all theme graphics, regardless of type.

Each theme has a particular **colour scheme** associated with it. Simply clicking the **Apply <Theme>** thumbnail applies the theme without altering the site's existing colour scheme. To apply a new theme along with its default colour scheme (thereby updating any graphics in the site that use scheme colours), choose **Apply With Colour Scheme** from the thumbnail's popup menu.

You can Undo any of these actions if you change your mind.

To move or resize a theme graphic:

- Drag the object to move it, or drag by its edge or corner handles to resize.

You can edit the text of individual theme graphics, and set various properties for a single theme graphic, or for all theme graphics of a particular type or set.

To edit one or more theme graphics:

1. Double-click the object. (If you're updating a type or set, choose a representative object.)
   OR
   Select the object and click its [T] **Edit** button, or right-click it and choose **Edit Theme Graphic...**.
2. Use the dialog tabs to set theme graphic properties. The actual properties you can edit depend on the type of theme graphic, but may include text, subtext, text fill colour(s), and font.
3. Click **OK** to apply changes.

Using the Gallery

The **Gallery** tab serves as a container for storing your own design objects (such as pictures, Flash banners, text blocks, even unlinked text frames or HTML fragments) you'd like to reuse in different web sites. It also includes sample designs and (when you install the *WebPlus 10 Resource CD*) is stocked with a wide variety of predesigned elements that you can customize and use as a starting point for your own designs. Once you've copied a design to the Gallery, it becomes available to any web site—simply open the Gallery!

To view the Gallery tab:

- The **Gallery** tab is by default docked with other tabs. If not displayed, go to **View>Studio Tabs** and select the **Gallery** tab.

The Gallery has two parts: (1) an upper **Categories** group and (2) a lower **Designs** group where you drag designs for storage. The Designs group shows a list of thumbnails representing the designs in the selected category.

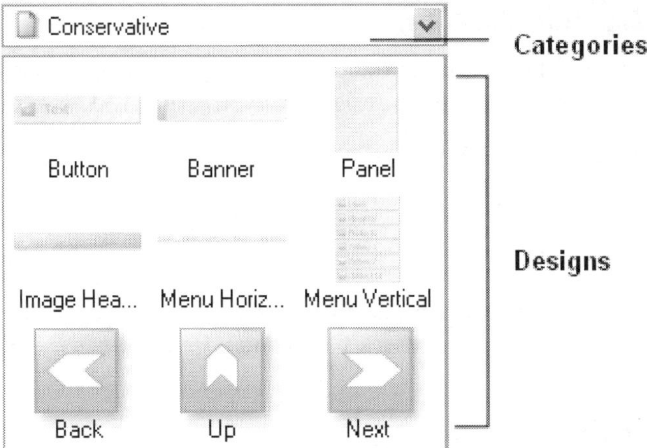

You can maintain your own collection of Gallery designs by adding and deleting items, with the option of naming individual elements to facilitate rapid access.

Each design in the design group can be deleted or renamed from a drop-down menu, accessible from the bottom right-hand corner of any design thumbnail.

To add, delete, or rename Gallery categories:

1. With the Gallery tab selected, click the **Options** button and choose **Add category...**, **Remove category**, or **Rename category...** from the drop-down list.

2. If adding a category, you need to name the category in a dialog. For removal or deletion, simply pick the category in advance of picking the option.

To move or copy an object into the Gallery:

1. Select the gallery category into which you want to add the object. Use the Categories drop-down menu for this.

2. To move, drag the object from the page and drop it in the category window. To copy, press the **Ctrl** key before starting to drag.

3. If the **Prompt to Rename** option is turned on, you'll be prompted to type a name for the design. (You can name or rename the design later, if you wish.) By default, unnamed designs are labelled as "Unnamed."

4. A thumbnail of the design appears in the Designs group, and its label appears below the design.

To use a design from the Gallery:

- Click its thumbnail in the design category and drag it out onto the page. The Gallery retains a copy of the design until you expressly delete it.

To delete a design from the Gallery:

- Select a design thumbnail, click on the drop-down button in the bottom-right corner (shown by hover over) and choose **Delete Design...** from the menu.

If you want the Gallery to present a confirmation dialog each time you delete a design, right-click on a design and check **Confirm on Delete**. Uncheck to bypass confirmation.

Naming designs

To rename a design:

- Hover over the design thumbnail, click on the drop-down icon and choose **Rename Design...** from the menu. Type the new name and click **OK**. The new name appears immediately underneath the design.

If you want the Gallery to prompt you for a name each time you drag in a new design, check **Prompt for Name** from the above menu. Uncheck to bypass the prompt.

Finding designs

To locate a design:

1. Click on the **Options** button on the Gallery tab and choose **Find Design....** from the menu.
2. Type the text to find and click **Find Next**. Starting from the first item displayed, WebPlus searches for the next design (if any) whose name or text includes the search text. The search spans all your Gallery categories.

Click **Find Next** to continue the search, or **Close** to exit.

Setting page and site properties

Your WebPlus site has its own general framework, consisting of the **site** itself; one or more **master pages**; and a number of individual **pages**. Each aspect of the framework has various **property** settings that contribute to the look and behaviour or your site when it's published. Whether you start with a WebPlus template or from scratch, you can choose whether to stick with the default property settings or alter them to suit your needs.

To view or change most property settings:

- (Site properties) Choose **Site Properties...** from the File menu. The Site Properties dialog appears.
- (Master page properties) Click the **Master Page Manager** button above the Master Pages window on the Site tab (or on the HintLine), or choose the item from the View menu. The Master Page Manager appears.
- (Page properties) Right-click the page in the workspace and choose **Page Properties....** Alternatively, on the Studio's **Site** tab, single-click to select the page in the Site Structure tree, right-click the page entry and choose **Page Properties...** (or choose the item from the Edit menu). The Page Properties dialog appears.

Setting page and file names

Each page has a **page name**, as shown in its entry in the Site tab's Site Structure tree, and a **file name**. Normally, after you've published the page as HTML, the page name appears as its **title** in the visitor's Web browser when the page is viewed; the file name is used to store the physical page. WebPlus assigns default names in series ("Page 1," "Page 2," etc.) as new pages are created.

For various reasons, you might want or need to change these properties for one or more pages. For example, you might want all the pages in a section (or even in the whole site) to display the same title. You can use the Page Properties dialog to change the visible page name, specify a different HTML title, and/or change the file name. As a site property, you can change the default file extension.

Leaving the page name or title undefined won't affect the performance of your site in any way.

To change page name, file name, and/or HTML title:

1. Right-click the page in the workspace and choose **Page Properties...**.
   OR

   Right-click the page entry in the Site tab's Site Structure tree and choose **Page Properties...** (or choose the item from the Edit menu).

2. On the dialog's Page tab, type a different page name if you wish. To use a different HTML title, enable the **Specify HTML title** button and type a different title. To use a different file name and/or extension, change the default name provided by clicking the **Change...** button.

To change the default file extension:

1. Choose **Site Properties...** from the File menu.

2. On the dialog's Options tab, select a different **Default file extension** if necessary.

Setting page size and alignment

Default site property settings for **Width** and **Height** determine the dimensions of master pages, and each master page in turn determines the size of pages that use it. A default site property setting for **alignment** (either Left or Centered) determines how page content lines up in a browser.

One of the first things you may want to do, when creating a new site from scratch, is to check the default dimensions and adjust them if necessary. You can also override the site setting for a given master page as needed. Individual pages that don't use a master page (for example, HTML pages you've imported) can have their own dimensions. You can adjust the dimension settings at any time—but as a rule, make changes before you've gone too far with laying out page elements!

In general, use a **Width** setting that will fit on a standard monitor (750 pixels is usually safe) and won't force users to scroll horizontally.

As for **Height**, allow enough vertical distance to let you lay out the objects on your longest page. It's OK to allow more space than you expect to fill. As each individual page is published to the Web, WebPlus will truncate the page either at the specified Height setting or just below the bottom element on each page/master page, whichever is less. In other words, there's no danger of blank space below your bottom element—but don't let elements run outside the indicated page dimensions.

WebPlus lets you select one or more master page objects, and have them **Attach to Bottom of Page** (available in Arrange menu). This means that objects which should belong to the base of the page such as copyright information, bottom navbars, or navigation buttons will **always** show on the bottom of the web page irrespective of page height.

To adjust page dimension settings:

- (Site defaults) Choose **Site Properties...** from the File menu. On the dialog's **Options** tab, select different **Width** and/or **Height** values to apply to master pages.
- (To override the site setting for a particular master page) Click the **Master Page Manager** button above the Master Pages window in the Site tab (or on the HintLine), or choose the item from the View menu. Select the master page from the window, click the **Properties** button and specify **Width** and/or **Height** values. The new values affect all pages using that master page.
- (For pages not using a master page) Right-click the page in the workspace and choose **Page Properties...**.
  OR
  Right-click the page entry in the Site tab and choose **Page Properties...** (or choose the item from the Edit menu). On the dialog's Page tab, select custom **Width** and/or **Height** values.
- (For specific or all pages) Select **Resize Page...** from the File menu. Select a specific or all pages from the drop-down menu and set the new **Width** and/or **Height** value for the page(s).

You can also change the default page alignment setting as a site property, or override it for a given page.

To adjust the page alignment setting:

- (Site default) Choose **Site Properties...** from the File menu. On the dialog's **Options** tab, select either "Left" or "Centered" in the **Default page alignment** drop-down menu.

- (To override the site setting for a particular page) Right-click the page in the workspace and choose **Page Properties....**
  OR
  Right-click the page entry in the Site tab and choose **Page Properties...** (or choose the item from the Edit menu). On the dialog's Page tab, change the "Use Site Setting" default to be either "Left" or "Centered" in the **Page Alignment** list.

Viewing and changing project information

WebPlus maintains basic properties and statistics for each project file.

To view or change project properties:

1. Choose **Site Properties...** from the File menu.
2. Click the Summary tab to view or change fields for Author, Keywords, Comments, Title, or Subject.
3. Click the Statistics tab to view key dates, etc.

For tracking version history, especially if layout work is being shared, you may wish to display current properties so they show up on the screen or on a printout. Properties you can insert include Site title, Filename, Author, Last Edit Time, Revision Count, and Page Count.

To insert project information in your text:

1. Select the Pointer tool and click in the text for an insertion point.
2. Choose **Information** from the Insert menu, then select **Site Info...** from the submenu. Select a property to insert and click **OK**.

If the project information changes, the information field in the text is automatically updated.

Add to Favourites

The favourites feature is used to include a graphical portrayal of your web site, a company logo, or other distinguishable symbol, to precede any bookmark stored in a web visitor's browser favourites.

An .ICO file must have been previously created to represent your site.

To create a favourites icon for your site:

1. Choose **Site Properties...** from the File menu.
2. Click the Favourites tab and check the **Show a favourites icon..** option.
3. **Browse** for an .ICO file, and in the Open dialog, select the file and click **Open**.

4. Check **Embed file** if you want to incorporate the icon file into your WebPlus project file.

5. (Optional) Set **Export Options** to define an exported file name and physical location. (See **Setting picture export options** on p. 129.).

Applying page transitions

Start or exit pages in a unique way with a page transition effect—just like in the movies! WebPlus allows you to set a transition effect for each page in your web site. An impressive collection of wipes, blinds, strips, bars, and many more, can be selected—try each one in turn and preview until you find one you like. Entry and exit transitions share the same effect types but differ in that the transition is applied when the web visitor initially loads the page (entry) or when leaving the page (exit).

If there's a particular transition you want to use throughout your web site, it can be applied to a master page. All other page assigned that master page will adopt the master page's transition unless the page overrides the master page setting (by setting another transition or none).

As a cautionary note, it's a good idea to use transitions sparingly. As with a lot of effects with a strong visual impact it's very easy for the effect to become tiresome after a while. It may also help to reduce the time over which the transition will be taking place.

WebPlus will prevent both an exit and entry transition occurring simultaneously between a first and a second web page. The exit transition on the first page is ignored.

To view page transitions you'll need to be running Internet Explorer as your Web browser.

To add a page transition to a master page:

1. Right-click a Master page icon in the Site tab's Master Page window and select **Properties...**.
   OR

   Click the **Master Page Manager** button above the Master Pages window of the Site tab (or on the HintLine), or choose the item from the View menu. In the Master Page Manager, select the master page and click **Properties**.

2. In the dialog, select the Page Transitions tab.

3. Choose either a Page Entry or Page Exit **Transition type** (or both) from their respective drop-down menus.
4. Set a suitable transition **Duration** (preview each transitions for the optimum duration).
5. Click **OK**.

To add (or remove) a page transition to a web page:

1. Right-click the page in the workspace and choose **Page Properties...**.
   OR

   In the Studio's Site tab, right-click to select the page in the Site Structure tree and choose **Page Properties...** (or choose the item from the Edit menu).
2. In the dialog, select the Transitions tab.
3. Check the **Override Master page** setting (this means the page will adopt its own transition) for Page Entry or Page Exit Transitions (or both) and select from the drop-down menu(s). Selecting "None" switched off an entry or exit transition.
4. Set a suitable **Duration**.

Redirecting pages

At some point in a web site's life, pages will be updated, added, reorganized or removed. Without WebPlus's page redirection, if you reorganize or remove pages, your returning web visitors who have bookmarked such pages on your site will receive the dreaded "404" Not Found error when trying to access the now missing page's bookmark.

Redirection of pages in WebPlus will jump the visitor from "old" pages to equivalent "live" pages to maintain a good level of a service. By keeping old pages alongside live pages for a period of time (instead of deleting them), you can redirect a visitor to anywhere you want. If there's no equivalent page (e.g., if your site has been completely overhauled), it makes sense to redirect to a new Home page for the new site.

To prevent old and new pages from cluttering up your Site Structure Tree (Site tab), make old pages children of your Home page (by drag drop over the Home page icon) and collapse the Home page tree.

Redirection is possible to a range of link destinations—typically another page in your site, or maybe an external web page, email address, local file, anchor, shopping cart, to name a few.

To add a page redirect from your web page:

1. Right-click the page in the workspace and choose **Page Properties....**
   OR

   In the Studio's Site tab, right-click to select the page in the Site Structure tree and choose **Page Properties...** (or choose the item from the Edit menu).
2. In the dialog, select the Redirect tab.
3. Click the link button which will provide a list of link destination types. (See **Adding hyperlinks and anchors** on p. 149). Select an option.
4. Set a suitable **Time delay**. This will allow your web visitor to read any relevant messages on the current page before redirection is attempted.
5. Click **OK**.

Using File Manager

The **File Manager** is especially useful if you want to view and manage your site structure by file name instead of by page title (by using the Site tab's Site Structure). It's therefore possible to reorganize the underlying file/folder structure without affected the page-based site structure.

The File Manager's structure is shown in tree form similar to that of Windows Explorer. In fact, like Explorer, you can perform various file management operations, e.g.

- Add, delete, move, or rename new folders
- Add files (images, HTML, or script files) to selected folders
- Rename or move files
- Display web page for any selected filename.
- Edit the Page Properties for any selected filename.

The file structure may also be familiar to you if specifying different **Web Export Options** for images. On export, images can be saved to a specific name and path. See **Setting Picture Export Options** on p. 129.

Adding search engine descriptors

Although they're optional, if you want to increase the likelihood that your Web site will be "noticed" by major Web search services, you should enter **search engine descriptors**. Search services maintain catalogues of Web pages, often compiled through the use of "crawlers" or other programs that prowl the Web collecting data on sites and their content. By including descriptive information and keywords, you'll assist these engines in properly categorizing your site. You can enter descriptors for the site as a whole and/or for individual pages.

It's also possible to use HTML tags in your HTML frames/tables to prioritize your page when retrieved in a user's Internet search engine.

To enter search engine descriptors:

1. (For the site) Choose **Site Properties...** from the File menu.
   OR
   (For a page) Right-click the page in the workspace or Site tab and choose **Page Properties...** (or choose the item from the Edit menu).
2. Click the dialog's **Search** tab.
3. In the top window, type in a brief description of your site. Although the description can be any length, the first ten words or so are the most important.
4. In the next window, enter any number of keywords (separated by commas) that you think fairly categorize your site. Put yourself in the place of a potential visitor. What keywords might they enter if they were searching for exactly what your site or page has to offer?
5. Check **Tell search engines how to index pages on this site** if you want to control how search engines index your web site. Use the two sub-options to allow or prevent search engines indexing the entire site (first option) or to allow indexing of all pages linked from the home page or index just the home page (second option). Check or uncheck for each option, respectively.
6. Set a language code for your site from the drop-down menu to identify your site's language use. Most user's Internet search engines will permit language specific searches for web pages, so your site will show in search results according to its language code setting.

HTML Heading tags for prioritized searching

Whether you're working with an HTML frame or HTML table, it's useful to know that any HTML assigned with the heading tags H1, H2, H3, and H4 will be prioritized in Internet search engines ahead of tags which are not heading tags (i.e., <p> paragraph tags).

To assign a heading tag to text in HTML frames or tables:

1. Select text in the frame or table.
2. From the Format menu, go to the **HTML tag** option and choose a heading tag (H1 is the highest priority and equates to Heading 1; H6 is the lowest priority). The tag is assigned to the text.

Using WebSafe Fonts Manager

The **WebSafe Fonts Manager** controls the system-wide list of WebSafe fonts available to WebPlus, ensuring that a web visitor will see your web site's text as intended. WebSafe fonts in WebPlus are a specially selected and configurable subset of fonts which are deemed to offer the best selection of fonts to maximize the chances that fonts match between your web site (during design) and your web visitors' computers (during browsing).

Generally speaking, it is advisable to keep to the standard list of WebSafe fonts unless you can be sure of font usage amongst your target audience. These fonts are always grouped at the top of the Font list on the Text context toolbar (click any frame, table, or artistic text to display). All WebSafe fonts are shown with a green tick, i.e.

A **WebSafe Fonts** dialog lets you decide if installed fonts are treated as WebSafe (the font is assumed to be installed on the web visitor's computer), rasterized on export (i.e. converted to bitmap), or if you're undecided, checked in the Layout Checker prior to publishing. If you do nothing (or forget to check), text using fonts not deemed WebSafe will be rasterized by default.

Changing WebSafe export options

In a more controlled environment such as a corporate Intranet you may be able to take the opportunity to increase the list of fonts which are considered to be WebSafe. Knowing the fonts used by your web visitor's (they may be a common set installed from a central server), you can afford to relax the subset of WebSafe fonts used. At a later date, it's probable that the WebSafe fonts will need to be managed.

To change an installed font to be WebSafe:

1. Select **WebSafe Fonts Manager...** from the Tools menu.
2. In the dialog, select a font labelled with a ? (a font for checking in Layout Checker) or [A] (a rasterized font) from the list.
3. In the **WebSafe Export Options** drop-down menu, select "Assume font is installed". This makes the selected font WebSafe (it will now show at the top of the Fonts list).
4. Click **OK**.

It is also possible to do the reverse and change a WebSafe font to rasterize on export, or be checked in Layout checker (in fact any combination will work). Check the fonts label in the dialog's Installed Fonts list and choose an appropriate export option.

Here's an example of three different fonts each labelled with different respective export options, i.e. "Assume font is installed", "Resolve in layout checker", and "Rasterize font on export".

Promotion via email

With a powerful design environment at your fingertips you might like to produce some stylish sales flyers, datasheets, or other information in relation to your web site or even completely independent of it. WebPlus's object creation capabilities (lines, QuickShapes, and text) coupled with its powerful colour and transparency control means that you can design a stylish page easily and then dispatch it via email.

- Design your page and select **Send Current Page as E-mail** from the File menu.

Updating and saving defaults

Object defaults are the stored property settings WebPlus applies to newly created objects, e.g. text, graphics, and frames. When you create text in your site, it will have default properties for font, size, colour, alignment, etc. New graphics will have default properties for line and fill colour, shade, pattern, etc. New frames will have default properties for margins, columns, etc. You can easily change the defaults for any type of object.

Default settings are always **local**—that is, any changed defaults apply to the current site and are automatically saved with it, so they're in effect next time you open that site. However, at any time you can use the **Save Defaults** command to record the current defaults as **global** settings that will be in effect for any new site you subsequently create.

To set local defaults for a particular type of object:

1. Create a single sample object and fine-tune its properties as desired—or use an existing object that already has the right properties. (For graphics, you can use a line, shape, or rectangle; all share the same set of defaults.)
2. Select the object that's the basis for the new defaults and choose **Update Object Default** from the Format menu.

Or, for line and fill colours, including line styles:

1. With no object selected, choose the required line and/or fill colours from the Colour or Swatches tab (see **Applying solid colours** on p. 117). Use the Line tab to set a default line weight, style, and corner shape.
2. Draw your object on the page, which will automatically adopt the newly defined default colours and styles.

You can also view and change the current default text properties in the Text Style Palette.

To view and change default text properties:

1. Choose **Text Style Palette...** from the Format menu.
2. Click **Default Text**, then click **Modify...** to view current settings.
3. Use the **Attributes** button to alter character, paragraph, or other properties.

To save all current defaults as global settings:

1. Choose **Save Defaults** from the Tools menu.

Click **OK** to confirm that you want new sites to use the current site's defaults.

Working with Text

4

Importing text from a file

Importing text from a word-processor file is the traditional way to create text content for Desktop Publishing layouts (but you can also create a story using **WritePlus**). If you use your current word processor (such as Microsoft Word) to create the text file for your site, you can import any number of files into one site. Each file becomes a **story** consisting of a self-contained section of text like a single article in a newspaper, which flows in a sequence of linked **text frames**.

To import text:

1. Choose **Text File...** from the Insert menu.
   OR
   Right-click a frame and choose **Text File...**. The **Open** dialog appears.
2. Select the format of the source file to be imported and locate the file itself. (See below for details on setting the preferred text import format.)
3. Check the "Retain Format" box to retain the source file's formatting styles. Uncheck the box to discard this information. In either case, WebPlus will preserve basic character properties like italic, bold, and underline, and paragraph properties like alignment (left, centre, right, justified).
4. Check the "Ignore Line Wrapping" box to ignore returns in the source text—that is, only if the file has been saved with a carriage return at the end of every line, and you want to strip off these extra returns. Otherwise, leave the box unchecked.
5. Click **OK**.

WebPlus will import the designated text into a text frame, either flowing text into a selected frame or creating a new frame.

Two special options exist to help you fit imported text into a series of frames. AutoFlow can automatically create text frames and pages until all the text has been imported; a Registry change is required to activate it. On the other hand, you can apply **AutoFit** (which fits text exactly to the available frame area) or use the frame's AutoFlow button at any time after the text has been imported. For details, see Fitting text to frames.

For details on changing frame column and margin settings, see **Creative frame setup and layout** on p. 74.

Understanding text frames

Typically, text in WebPlus goes into **text frames**, which work equally well as containers for single words, standalone paragraphs, or multipage articles or chapter text. You can also use **artistic text** (see p. 80) for standalone text with special effects, or **table text** (see **Creating text-based tables** on p. 95) for row-and-column displays.

What's a text frame?

A text frame is effectively a mini-page, with:

- Optional preceding and following frames
- Text and optional **inline images** that flow through the frame (from the previous frame and on to the next).

The text in a frame is called a **story**.

- When you move a text frame, its story text moves with it.
- When you resize a text frame, its story text reflows to the new dimensions.

Frames can be linked so that a single story continues from one frame to another. But text frames can just as easily stand alone. Thus in any Web site, you can create text in a single frame, spread a story over several frames, and/or include many independent frame sequences, e.g.

When you select a frame you'll see its bounding box (see Frame 1 in example), indicated by a grey border line plus corner and edge handles, and (if you clicked with the Pointer tool) a blinking insertion point in the frame's text. In this mode, you can edit the text with the Pointer tool. As in a word processor, double-clicking selects a word, and triple-clicking selects a paragraph.

HTML or Creative frames

Two types of frame can be applied to the page—the HTML text frame and the Creative text frame. These can be compared easily in the following table.

	HTML frames	**Creative frames**
Searchable by search engines	✓	×
Script and form insertion for generating dynamic content	✓	×
Margins and column guides	×	✓
Breaks (column, page, and frame)	×	✓
Resize/move frame	✓	✓
Crop frame	×	✓
Rotate frame	×	✓[1]
Frame linking	×	✓
Columns	×	✓
Export as text	✓	✓[2]
Copy and paste exported text	✓	✓
Apply fill and line colour	✓	✓
HTML-compliant Styles	✓	×
Transparency	×	✓[1]
Borders	×	✓[1]
Warp	×	✓[1]
2D/3D Filter Effects	×	✓[1]
Instant 3D	×	✓[1]

[1] If applied, will export frame as a graphic.

[2] Only if rotate, crop, transparency, a border or a filter effect is not applied.

HTML-compliant styles means that you can format text in your HTML frame using heading styles (tags) from H1, H2, .., to H6. The styles can be assigned from **Text>HTML Tag** on the Format menu. An advantage of this is that text applied with Heading styles are given priority in Internet search engines (H1 tag is the highest priority). See **Adding search engine descriptors** on p. 62 for more details.

So how do you tell the difference between an HTML and Creative frame? Simply, HTML frames will always possess dark blue corner/edge handles when selected, while a Creative frame's handles will show as grey.

To select only the frame (no insertion point):

- Click the frame's bounding box. When only the frame is selected, you can move it more easily.

To move a text frame:

- Drag the frame's bounding box.
  OR
- Use the X or Y options in the Transform tab.

To resize a text frame:

- In any selection mode, drag a corner or edge handle.
  OR
- Use the W or H options in the Transform tab.

Creating frames

You add frames to a page as you would any other object. You can resize any frame, but cannot alter its basic shape.

To create a frame:

1. Click either the **HTML Frame Tool** or the **Creative Frame Tool** button from the Insert flyout on the Standard Objects toolbar (see **HTML or Creative frames** on p. 71).
2. Click on the page or pasteboard to create a new frame at a default size or drag to adjust the frame's dimensions.

You can use the **Update Object Default** from the Format menu to set properties for future new frames you create. See **Updating and saving defaults** on p. 65.

To delete a frame:

- Select the frame object and press the **Delete** key. (If there's a selection point in the text, pressing **Delete** will remove characters after the cursor.)
  OR
- With or without an insertion point, choose **Delete Object** from the Edit menu.

Putting text into a frame

You can put text into an HTML or Creative frame in one of several ways. For HTML frames, text will be converted to compliant HTML code.

1. WritePlus story editor:

- To start **WritePlus**, right-click on a frame and choose **Edit Story** (shortcut **Ctrl+E**).
  OR
  Click the **WritePlus** button on the Frame context toolbar.

This opens the WebPlus integrated story editor—useful for typing, formatting, and proofing large amounts of text. If the frame already contains text, it is automatically loaded into WritePlus for editing. (See **Editing text with WritePlus** in WebPlus help.)

2. Importing text:

- Right-click on a frame and choose **Text File...** (shortcut **Ctrl+T**) to import text.

If there's an insertion point in existing text, the new text appears at that point. If there's a range of text selected, the new text replaces it. If only the frame is selected, the new text is inserted at the beginning of the story.

If you want to create a simple document with just one story running from page to page, use the **Text File...** command with no frame selected. WebPlus automatically adds frames matching the underlying page layouts you've set up. The **AutoFlow** option can add pages as needed, until all your text has been imported.

3. Typing into the frame:

- Select the Pointer tool, then click for an insertion point to type text straight into a frame, or edit existing text. (See **Editing text on the page** on p. 81.)

4. Pasting via the Clipboard:

- Select the Pointer tool and click for an insertion point in the text, then press **Ctrl+V**.

5. Drag and drop:

- Select text (e.g. in a word processor file), then drag it onto the WebPlus page.

If you drop onto a selected a frame, the text is pasted inline after existing text. Otherwise, a new frame is created for the text.

When designing and testing your frame layout, use **Fill with Placeholder Text** on the Insert menu to quickly populate frames with text.

Creative frame setup and layout

The **frame layout** of a Creative frame controls how text will flow in the frame. The frame can contain multiple **columns**. When a frame is selected, its column margins appear as dashed grey guide lines when values for column blinds and margins are defined (Text Frames must also be switched on in the View menu).

Note that unlike the page margin and row/column guides, which serve as layout guides for placing page elements, the frame column guides actually determine how text flows within each frame. Text won't flow outside the column guides.

You can drag the column guides or use a dialog to adjust the top and bottom **column blinds** and the left and right **column margins**.

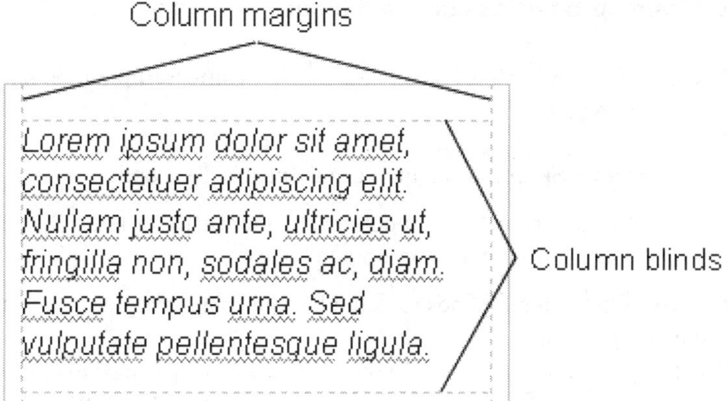

To edit frame properties directly:

- Select the frame, then drag column guide lines to adjust the boundaries of the column.

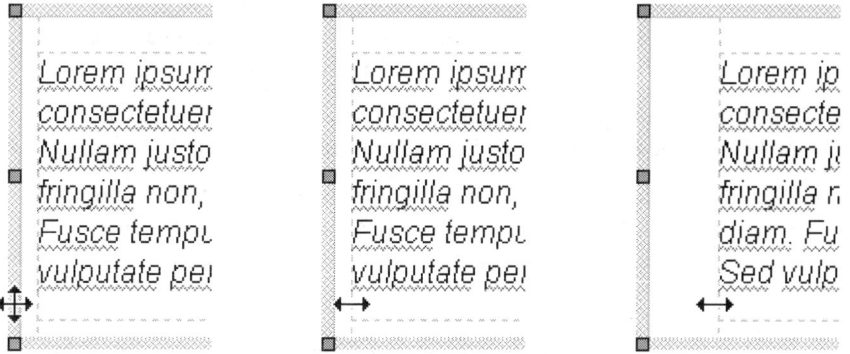

The illustration above shows how the cursor changes to show when you're (1) over the frame's bounding box or (2) over one of its column boundaries. In (3), the left frame margin has been dragged in slightly. Notice how paragraph indents are preserved relative to the margin guide.

To edit frame properties using a dialog:

1. Select the Creative frame and click the **Frame Setup** button on the Frame context toolbar.
   OR
   Choose **Frame Setup...** from the Format menu's **Text** option.
2. In the dialog, set the number of columns, gutter (gap), or left/right frame margins, enter values in the appropriate boxes.
3. To change the column blinds (top and bottom frame margins), click a cell in the table and enter a new value.
   Hint: If the frame has more than one column, you only need to enter top/bottom values for the first one. Then click **Top** and/or **Bottom** to repeat the entries instantly in the cells below.

Story flow through Creative frames

Stories cannot flow between HTML frames, as they do not support linking (text can only overflow a single frame).

You can have just one Creative frame on its own, or you can have many frames. Frames can be connected in linked **sequences**.

The **story** associated with a given frame sequence flows through the first frame on to the next and keeps flowing into frames in the link sequence.

A key difference from a word processor is that WebPlus does not normally add or remove frames according to the amount of text. The text simply flows until the text runs out (and some frames are left empty), or the frames run out (and some text is left over).

If there is still more text to go after filling the last frame, WebPlus stores it in an invisible **overflow area**, remembering that it's part of the story text—the **Link** button on the last frame of the sequence is displayed. If you later add more frames or reduce the size of text in a frame, the rest of the story text is flowed in.

If the text runs out before the last frame, you have some empty frames. These frames will be filled with text if you add more text to the story, or if you increase the size of the story text.

WebPlus keeps track of multiple linked frame sequences, and lets you flow several stories in the same site. The Text Manager (accessed via the Tools menu) provides an overview of all stories and lets you choose which one you want to edit.

AutoFlow

When importing text, it's a good idea to take advantage of the **AutoFlow** feature, which will automatically create text frames and pages until all the text has been imported. This way, enough frames are created to display the whole story. Then you can gauge just how much adjustment will be needed to fit the story to the available "real estate" in your site. You can make the major changes first, then proceed to the fine-tuning.

Making text fit the frame

To make your text fit within a frame you can use the **AutoFit** button, or incrementally increase or decrease the frame text (with **Enlarge Story Text** or **Shrink Story Text**). All buttons are hosted on the frame's context toolbar.

Linking Creative frames

When selected, a text frame includes a **Link** button at the bottom right which allows you to import text files or control how the frame's story flows to following frames. The icon inside each frame's Link button denotes the state of the frame and its story text:

No Overflow
The frame is not linked to a following frame (it's either a standalone frame or the last frame in a sequence) and the end of the story text is visible.

Overflow
The frame is not linked (either standalone or last frame) and there is additional story text in the overflow area.

Continued
The frame is linked to a following frame. The end of the story text may be visible, or it may flow into the following frame.
Note: The button icon will be red if the final frame of the sequence is overflowing, or green if there's no overflow.

There are two basic ways to set up a linked sequence of frames:

- You can link a sequence of empty frames, then import the text.
  OR
- You can import the text into a single frame, then create and link additional frames into which the text automatically flows.

When frames are created by the **AutoFlow** option when importing text, they are automatically linked in sequence.

To create a link or reorder the links between existing frames, you can use the **Link** button or the controls on the Frame context toolbar. Remember to watch the cursor, which changes to indicate these operations...

To link the selected frame to another frame as the next frame:

- Click the frame's **Link** button.
  OR

  Select the frame, then click the **Link Frame** button on the Frame context toolbar.
- Click with the Textflow cursor on the frame to be linked to. Only empty frames are valid frames to link to.

To unlink the selected frame from the sequence:

- Click the **Unlink Frame** button on the Frame context toolbar.
  OR
  Click on the frame's **Link** button, then click with the Textflow cursor on the same frame.

Story text remains with the "old" frames. For example, if you detach the second frame of a three-frame sequence, the story text remains in the first and third frames, which are now linked into a two-frame story. The detached frame is always empty.

If you click on a frame's **Link** button, and then change your mind about linking or unlinking, press the **Esc** key or click on a blank area of the page or pasteboard to cancel.

To navigate from frame to frame:

- Click the **Previous Frame** or **Next Frame** button on the Frame context toolbar.

Graphic properties of frames

Like graphics, all frames have **line** and **fill** properties—initially an outline of zero weight and a clear fill. Although HTML frames cannot possess transparency, Creative frames can (initially set to None). As with graphics, you can edit these properties, for example adding a grey or light-coloured fill as shading behind a frame's text. You can also import images **inline** with frame text.

Note that the text inside a frame can take a solid colour, but doesn't have line and fill properties as such—for fancy line/fill effects with text, you can employ **artistic text** (see p. 80).

Controlling overflowing text (HTML frames)

As HTML frames have to comply with HTML standards, they are not capable of linking stories (as for Creative frames). As a result, a decision has to be made about what happens in the event of overflowing text. Overflowing HTML frames are clearly indicated—when selected, they will show an **Overflow** button at the bottom right of the frame.

If you see this, you can choose to leave the text **Hidden**, let it **Overflow**, or let all the text be viewable with the help of a scroll bar.

To control overflowing text:

1. Select your overflowing HTML text frame.
2. Right-click on your frame, and go to **Format>Overflowing text** and choose:

   - **Hidden** - The frame as it is displayed on your page will be shown in a browser. Text will continue to be hidden.
   - **Overflow** - The frame will overflow (be extended) to allow all text within the frame to be shown.
   - **Scroll bar** - A navigation scroll bar is displayed permanently but will be greyed out if text does not overflow.
   - **Auto** - A navigation scroll bar is displayed only when text overflows the frame.

It's always a good idea to preview your HTML frames (via Preview in Window or via your browser)—especially if **Overflow** is selected.

Using artistic text

Artistic text is standalone text you type directly onto a page. Especially useful for headlines, pull quotes, and other special-purpose text, it's easily formatted with the standard text tools but has some artistic advantages over frame text. For example, you can initially "draw" artistic text at a desired point size, and drag it to adjust the size later. And unlike the characters in a text frame, an artistic text object can take different line styles, fills (including gradient and Bitmap fills), and transparency for stunning pictorial effects. You can even flip artistic text and it will remain editable!

Here are other similarities and differences between **frame text** and artistic text.

- With artistic text, as with frame text, you can vary **character and paragraph properties**, apply named **text styles**, edit text in **WritePlus**, access it with the Text Manager, track font usage with the Resource Manager, embed **inline images**, apply **filter effects**, and use proofing options such as AutoSpell/Spell Checker, Proof Reader, and Thesaurus.
- However, you cannot import text from a file. And because artistic text doesn't flow or link the way frame text does; the Frame context toolbar's text-fitting functions aren't applicable.

To create artistic text:

1. Choose the A **Artistic Text Tool** from the Tools toolbar's Artistic Text flyout.
2. Click anywhere on the page for an insertion point using a default point size, or drag to specify a particular size as shown here.

3. Set initial text properties as needed before typing, using the Text context toolbar, Format menu, or right-click (choose **Text Format>**).
4. Type normally to enter text.

Once you've created an artistic text object, you can select, move, resize, delete, and copy it just as you would with a text frame. Solid colours, gradient/Bitmap fills and transparency can all be applied.

To resize an artistic text object:

- Drag the object's handles to resize it while maintaining the object's proportions. To resize freely, hold down the **Shift** key while dragging.

To edit artistic text:

- Select a range of text by dragging. Double-click to select a word, or triple-click to select a paragraph.

Now you can type new text, apply character and paragraph formatting, edit the text in WritePlus, apply proofing options, and so on.

With artistic text, the **vertical alignment** setting anchors a particular part of the object—for example, a "top" setting anchors the top line and forces new text to come in below, while a "bottom" setting anchors the bottom (most recent) line and pushes previous lines up as you type new lines.

Please see WebPlus help for details on how to apply and edit artistic text on a path.

Editing text on the page

You can use the Pointer tool to edit **frame text**, **table text**, or **artistic text** directly. On the page, you can select and enter text, set paragraph indents and tab stops, change text properties, apply text styles, and use Find and Replace. For editing longer stories, and for more advanced options, choose WritePlus.

Selecting and entering text

To edit text on the page:

- Select the Pointer tool, then click or drag in the text frame. A standard insertion point appears at the click position, or a range of text is selected, ready for the text to be edited.

Lorem ipsum dolor sit amet, consectetuer adipiscing elit. Nullam justo ante, ultricies ut, fringilla non, sodales ac, diam. Fusce tempus urna. Sed vulputate pellentesque

Lorem ipsum dolor sit amet, consectetuer adipiscing elit. Nullam justo ante, ultricies ut, fringilla non, sodales ac, diam. Fusce tempus urna. Sed vulputate pellentesque

Tip: You can double-click to select a word, or triple-click to select a paragraph.

To start a new paragraph:

- Press **Enter**.

To start a new line:

- Press Shift+Enter. The line is created within the same paragraph (using a "line break" or "soft return")

The following two options apply only to frame text. You can use these shortcuts or choose the items from the **Insert>Break** submenu.

To flow text to the next column (Column Break):

- Press Ctrl+Enter.

To flow text to the next frame (Frame Break):

- Press Alt+Enter.

To switch between insert mode and overwrite mode:

- Press the **Insert** key.

To repeat a text action:

- Choose **Repeat** from the Edit menu, or press **Ctrl+Y**.

For example, if you've applied new formatting to one paragraph, you can click in another paragraph and use the **Repeat** command to apply the same formatting there.

Copying, pasting and moving text

You can easily copy frame text and paste into the same or a different text frame. Text stored on the clipboard can additionally be pasted into a new frame.

Drag and drop support for frame text allows text to be moved into a different location within the same frame or a different text frame in your site.

To copy and paste text:

1. Select the text to be copied.
2. Select **Copy** from the Edit menu. This places the text onto the clipboard.
3. Place an insertion point in a different location in your story or artistic text.
4. Select **Paste** from the Edit menu.

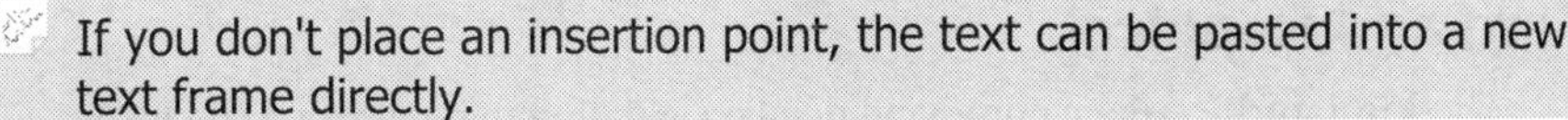
If you don't place an insertion point, the text can be pasted into a new text frame directly.

To move text by drag and drop (text frames only):

1. Select the text to be moved.
2. Hover over the selected text and hold your mouse button down. A cursor is shown.
3. Move the cursor to the location (in the same or different frame) you wish to place the text—an insertion point should be displayed.
4. Release the mouse button to place your text.

Setting paragraph indents

When a text frame is selected, markers on the horizontal ruler indicate the left indent, first line indent, and right indent of the current paragraph. You can adjust the markers to set paragraph indents, or use a dialog.

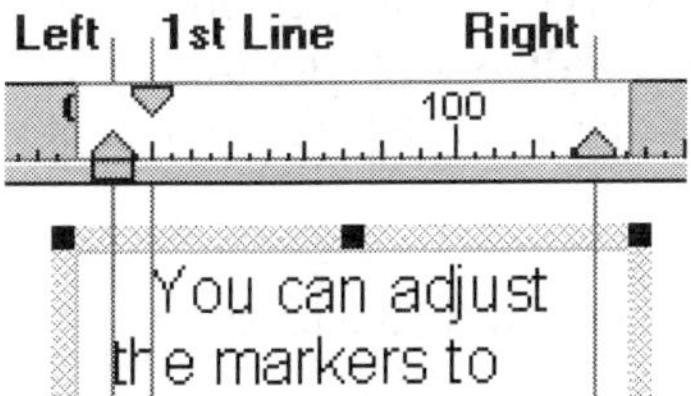

- The **Left** indent is set in relation to the frame's left margin.
- The **1st line** indent is in relation to the left indent.
- The **Right** indent is in relation to the frame's right margin.

For details on setting frame margins, see **Creative Frame setup and layout** on p. 74.

To set the indents of the current paragraph:

- Drag the appropriate ruler marker(s).
  OR
- To adjust indent settings numerically, choose **Text>Paragraph...** from the Format menu (or **Text Format>Paragraph...** from the right-click menu). You can enter values for Left, Right, 1st Line, or Hanging indents.

Find and Replace

The **Find and Replace** command displays a dialog that lets you search site text for words or parts of words. You can search text in all stories, or just the currently selected text object or story.

- Choose **Find & Replace...** from the Edit menu.

Setting text properties

WebPlus gives you a high degree of control over the fine points of typographic layout, whether you're working with **frame text**, **table text**, or **artistic text**.

To apply basic text formatting:

1. Select the text.
2. Use buttons on the Text context toolbar to change font, point size, font style, and paragraph alignment.
   OR
   Right-click the text and choose **Text Format**, then select from the submenu: **Character...**, **Paragraph...**, **Bullets and Numbering...**, or **Vertical Alignment**. (You can also select these items from the Format menu.)
   OR
   Use the **Character tab** to adjust point size, width, letter spacing (tracking), leading, and advance.

By default, text on your published Web pages is set to vary in size depending on the visitor's browser setting. If you wish, you can override this as a global option in WebPlus, so that text will appear in the browser at exactly the same point sizes used in your layouts. To check or change the setting, choose **Site Properties...** from the File menu. On the Options tab, check **Force absolute text size** to override the variable-text default.

Default text properties

Default text properties are the settings used for text you type into any new text object. You can change these settings directly from selected text, or using the Text Style Palette. The Palette has the advantage of letting you review all the settings at a glance. (For more on setting defaults, see **Updating and saving defaults** on p. 65.)

To change default text properties:

1. Create a single sample of text and fine-tune its properties as desired—or use existing text that already has the right properties.
2. Select the text or container and choose **Update Text Default** from the Format or right-click and choose **Format>**.
   OR
3. Choose **Text Style Palette...** from the Format menu.
4. Click **Default Text**, then click **Modify...** to view current settings.
5. Use the **Attributes** button to alter character, paragraph, or other properties.

Update Text Default will only apply to the current document and no other documents—use **Tools>Save Defaults** to apply the default to all subsequent documents.

WebPlus will preserve the formatting of imported word-processor text. If you've imported or pasted some text and want to apply different formatting, you can first reset the text to use the default text properties.

To clear custom formatting (restore plain/default text properties):

- Select a range of text and choose **Remove Text Formatting** from the Format menu (or press **Ctrl+Shift+Z**).

Using text styles

It's a good idea to establish the main text and graphic formatting to be used in your site early in the creative process. WebPlus facilitates this by letting you define named **text styles**. A text style is a set of character and/or paragraph attributes saved as a group. When you apply a style to text, you apply the whole group of attributes in just one step. For example, you could define named paragraph styles for particular layout elements, such as "Heading," "Sidebar," or "Body Text," and character styles to convey meaning, such as "Emphasis," "Price," or "Date Reference." Using styles not only speeds the task of laying out a site but ensures consistency and ease of updating.

Paragraph styles and character styles

A **paragraph style** is a complete specification for the appearance of a paragraph, including all its font and paragraph format attributes. Every paragraph in WebPlus has a paragraph style associated with it.

- WebPlus includes one built-in paragraph style called "**Normal**" with a specification consisting of generic attributes including left-aligned, 12pt Times New Roman. Initially, the "Normal" style is the default for any new paragraph text you type. You can modify the "Normal" style by redefining any of its attributes, and create any number of new styles having different names and attributes.

- Applying a paragraph style to text updates all the text in the paragraph except sections that have been locally formatted. For example, a single word marked as bold would remain bold when the paragraph style was updated.

A **character style** includes only font attributes (such as font name, point size, bold, italic, etc.), and you apply it at the character level—that is, to a range of selected characters—rather than to the whole paragraph.

- Typically, a character style applies emphasis (such as italics, bolding or colour) to whatever underlying font the paragraph already uses; the assumption is that you want to keep that underlying font the same. That's why WebPlus includes a built-in character style with the name **"Default Paragraph Font,"** which has no specified attributes but basically means "whatever font the paragraph style already uses." Suppose a paragraph uses a style called "Body," and the "Body" style uses regular 10pt Arial. Then the "Default Paragraph Font" style for that particular paragraph means regular 10pt Arial.

- The "Default Paragraph Font" style comes in handy if you have applied local formatting but then decide to restore the original text attributes for the paragraph. (You can think of it as a sort of "Revert to Unaltered Text" command.) Let's take the above example of a paragraph using the "Body" style, and suppose several words have been bolded. As noted earlier, reapplying the "Body" style to the paragraph would not undo the local bold marking. However, selecting the paragraph and applying the "Default Paragraph Font" style would set all the text back to regular 10pt Arial.
- As with paragraph styles, you can define any number of new character styles using different names and attributes. Custom character styles don't usually include a specific font name or point size, but there's no rule against including them.

Working with named styles

Normal The named style of the currently selected text appears in the **Styles** box on the Text context toolbar. The box may show a character style (if one is applied locally); otherwise it indicates the paragraph style. You can use either the Styles box or a dialog to apply a particular style to existing text, modify an existing style, or define a new style.

To apply a named style:

1. Using the Pointer tool, click in a paragraph (if applying a paragraph style) or select a range of text (if applying a character style). If you apply a paragraph style, it will be applied to the whole paragraph regardless of the amount of text selected. If you've selected text in more than one paragraph, the change takes place in all selected paragraphs.
2. Click the down arrow on the **Styles** box (on the Text context toolbar) and select the style name in the drop-down list.
   OR
   Choose **Text Style Palette...** from the Format menu, select a style name, and click **Apply**. The paragraph or selected text takes on the properties of the named style.

To update a named style using the properties of existing text:

1. Make any desired changes to some text that uses the named style as shown in the Styles box.
2. Choose **Update Text Style** from the Format menu.
   OR
   Click the arrow on the Styles box and select the current style name again from the list. Click **OK** to confirm the option to "Update the style to reflect recent changes."

All text using the named style, throughout the site, takes on the new properties.

To define a new style using the properties of existing text:

1. Format the text as desired.
2. To define a character style, select a range of reformatted text. To define a paragraph style, deselect text but leave a blinking cursor (insertion point) within the newly formatted section.
3. Type a new style name into the Styles box and press **Enter**.

The new style is defined with the properties of the selected text.

New styles in WebPlus are actually just modified styles, stored under new names. Every new style is derived from a previously defined **base style**, and so consists of all the base style's unchanged attributes as well as any attributes you've redefined.

To modify an existing style or define a new one using a dialog:

1. Choose **Text Style Palette...** from the Format menu.
2. To modify an existing style, select the style name and click **Modify...**.
   OR
   To create a new style, click **Create...**.
3. Use the **Style Properties** dialog to define (or change) the style name, base style, and following style. Click the **Attributes** button to access dialogs that let you specify any text attributes you want to include in the style definition.
4. Click **OK** to accept style properties, or **Cancel** to abandon changes.
5. Click **Apply** to update text, or click **Close** to maintain the style in the site for future use.

To import one or more styles from another WebPlus file:

1. Choose **Text Style Palette...** from the Format menu.
2. Click the **Import...** button and use the dialog to locate the file from which styles should be imported, and the specific style(s) to be imported.
3. Normally, new or updated styles are in effect only for the current site; they are saved with the project, but don't carry over to new sites. You can even save an empty project and the defined styles will be saved along with it! If you wish, you can use **Tools>Save Defaults** to record the set of styles (along with other defaults) as a global setting so it will remain in effect for future sites. For information, see .

Importing styles

When you use the **Insert>Text File...** command to import text from a word-processor file, you can choose whether or not to retain the source file's named styles.

- Check **Retain Format** in the Import Text dialog if you want WebPlus to import and retain these styles. Any text not tagged with a style will be marked with the "Normal" style as used in your site.
- Uncheck **Retain Format** to discard styles; WebPlus will mark all text with the "Normal" style, as for unstyled text in the case above.

Adjusting letter spacing

The spacing between characters in a paragraph can have a subtle effect on the viewer. WebPlus lets you experiment with the letter spacing of text. The normal value is expressed as 0%. Increase the value to spread text apart, and reduce it to tighten letter spacing. Letter spacing variations are preserved when you publish the Web page.

To adjust letter spacing between characters:

1. Select a range of text with the Pointer tool.
2. Display the Character tab and choose a value from the AV **Spacing** drop-down list box, or type in a new value.
   OR
   Right-click the text and choose **Text Menu>Text Format>Character...** (or choose **Character...** from the Format menu), then select the **Character Spacing** tab. Set the Spacing value to "Expanded" or "Condensed," and select a point value in the **By:** list box. To enter a relative (percent) value, uncheck the **Absolute** box.

Inserting a symbol

You can insert symbol characters using either the Insert menu or (for common symbols) keyboard shortcuts.

As a rule for Web page use, don't employ symbols outside the standard character set, or in non-standard fonts.

To insert a symbol character using the Insert menu:

1. Select the Pointer tool and click in the text for an insertion point.
2. Choose **Symbol...** from the Insert menu, and select a symbol name from the submenu.
3. If you need a symbol not shown on the submenu, select **Other...** to display an **Insert Symbol** dialog. The dialog remains open so you can continue editing in the workspace as you select symbols.
    - Select a **Font** to display its full character set, and then scroll the font table to view characters. You can choose from the **Subset** list to jump to a particular range within the character set.
    - Click any individual character (or select it while browsing using the arrow keys on your keyboard) to view the character's name and Unicode Index at the bottom of the dialog. You can also enter any Unicode hex value and click **Go** to jump to that particular character in the current font.
    - To insert a character into your text, double-click it (or select it and click **Insert**).

The memory row below the font table keeps track of characters you've recently inserted. Double-click any character in the row to insert it again.

Trouble inserting a character? Check your insertion point to ensure it is still placed in your chosen text position.

Inserting user details

You can take advantage of the User Details dialog to store frequently-used or -updated user information so you don't need to keep re-entering it—think of how often a mobile phone number or email address may change over time! The dialog lets you review all your User Details at a glance, and will update fields directly.

To review or change User Details:

1. Choose **Set User Details...** from the Tools menu.
2. Enter new information into the spaces on the **Business**, **Home**, or **Custom** tab.

The **Custom** tab of the User Details dialog includes blank, re-nameable fields where you can enter any information you may frequently need to "plug into" your sites.

To insert a User Detail field:

1. Select the Pointer tool and click in the text for an insertion point.
2. Choose **Information** from the Insert menu, then select **User Details...** from the submenu. Select a User Detail.

To update fields:

- Enter new information in the User Details dialog (via **Tools>Set User Details**).
- Click the **Update** button to automatically update any altered field currently placed in your site. This field will remain linked to User Details until it is deleted.

Working with Tables

5

Creating text-based tables

Tables are ideal for presenting text and data in a variety of easily customizable row-and-column formats, with built-in spreadsheet capabilities.

Quantity	Description	Code
12	Geraniums	34W-6YY
3	Plant Posts (small))	44X-123

Each cell in a table behaves like a mini-frame. There are many similarities (and several key differences) between **frame text** and table text.

- With table text, you can vary **character and paragraph properties**, apply named **text styles**, embed **inline images**, apply text colour fills, and use proofing options such as AutoSpell/Spell Checker, Proof Reader, and Thesaurus.
- However, tables don't support importing text from a file, editing text with WritePlus, or viewing text from within the Text Manager—table text also doesn't flow or link the way frame text does; the Frame context toolbar's text-fitting functions aren't applicable.
- Tables also have a number of unique features like **AutoFormat**, **number formatting**, **formula insertion**, **calendar insertion**, **QuickClear**, and **QuickFill** for rapid editing and revision.

HTML or Creative tables

Two types of table can be applied to the WebPlus page—the HTML table and the Creative table. These can be compared easily in the following table—some features can be applied to both, or just to one or the other. The features listed above apply to both table types.

	HTML tables	**Creative tables**
Searchable by search engines (Google, etc.)	✓	✗
Script and form insertion for generating dynamic content	✓	✗
Resize/move table	✓	✓
Crop table	✗	✗
Rotate table	✗	✓[1]
Rotate table text (in cell)	✗	✓[1]
Apply fill and border colour	✓	✓
HTML-compliant Styles	✓	✗
Transparency	✗	✓[1]
Borders	✗	✓[1]
Warp	✗	✓[1]
2D/3D Filter effects	✗	✓[1]
Instant 3D	✗	✓[1]

[1] If applied, will export table as a graphic.

HTML-compliant styles means that you can format text in your HTML table using heading styles (tags) from H1, H2, .., to H6. The styles can be assigned from **Text>HTML Tag** on the Format menu. An advantage of this is that text applied with Heading styles is retrieved in Internet search engines (H1 tag is the highest priority). See **Adding search engine descriptors** on p. 62 for more details.

So how do you tell the difference between an HTML and Creative table? Simply, HTML tables will always possess dark blue corner/edge handles when selected, while a Creative table's handles will show as grey.

To create a table:

1. Choose either the **HTML Table Tool** or **Creative Table Tool** from the Insert flyout on the Standard Objects toolbar, and click on the page or pasteboard, or drag to set the table's dimensions. The Create Table dialog appears with a selection of preset table formats shown in the **Format:** window.
2. Step through the list to preview the layouts and select one. To begin with a plain table, select **[Default]**.
3. Click **OK**.

The new table appears on the page, and the Table context toolbar appears to assist with entering and formatting spreadsheet data.

WebPlus treats table text in three ways: as **numbers**, **formulas**, or **ordinary text**.

- **Numbers:** WebPlus can format numbers in special ways. See **Formatting numbers** on p. 102.
- **Formulas:** WebPlus will treat any text entry beginning with an equal symbol (=) as a formula. Formulas can be formatted the same as numbers. See **Inserting formulas** on p. 104.
- **Ordinary text:** Any other text entry, i.e. one that doesn't begin with "=".

To modify an HTML or Creative table, please see **Manipulating tables** on p. 98.

HTML tables and dynamic content

If you want to use "intelligent" tables in WebPlus you'll need to work with HTML tables exclusively. The term "intelligent" means that the table as a whole (or a specific table cell) can either dynamically generate content or can have its appearance altered within table cells. Information could be gathered from a local database or generated by a script (perhaps the result of calculation of cell contents). Either way, an HTML fragment (containing the programming/script code) can be placed into one or more table cells, giving that cell the ability to generate dynamic content.

This complex subject is described in more detail in **Attaching HTML code** on p. 166, where some typical uses are also listed.

Manipulating tables

Once you've created a table, you can select, move, resize, delete, and copy it as an object, just as you would with a text frame.

To manipulate the table object:

- To select the table object, click its bounding box. Now you can resize it like a text frame by dragging a corner or side handle, or move it by dragging an edge.

- To delete the table object, select it and press the **Delete** key (you can also choose **Delete Object** from the Edit menu).
  OR
  Select any part of its text and choose **Delete** from the Table menu (**Table>Delete** from the right-click menu), then **Table** from the submenu.

- To duplicate the table object and its text, first make sure no text is selected (an insertion point is OK), then use the **Copy** and **Paste** commands. As a shortcut, select the object and drag with the **Ctrl** key down.

Other operations involve selecting text within the table, or parts of the table. Within each cell, you can click for an insertion point or drag to select a range of text. You can also drag to select multiple cells, rows, or columns, which in effect selects all the text in that region. Once you've made a selection, you can edit text in the table and modify the structure and appearance of the table and/or its components.

To select and edit text in cells, rows, and columns:

- To select a cell, click for an insertion point or drag to select text. To select more than one cell, click in one cell and drag across the others.

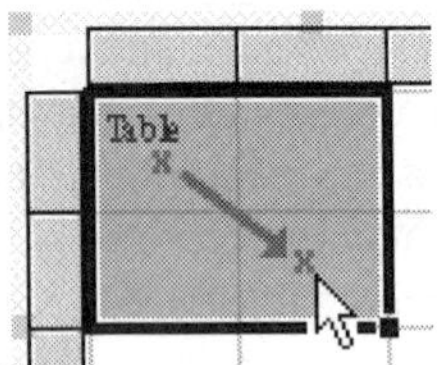

- To move between cells, use the keyboard arrow keys. You can also press **Tab** to move to the cell in the next column, and **Shift+Tab** to move to the cell in the previous column.

- To enter text, simply type into a cell at the insertion point. You can also type or edit text via the Table context toolbar's edit field.

  Click the ✓ **Accept** button to update the selected cell. Click ✕ **Cancel** to reset the edit field to the previous cell text. Cells expand vertically as you type to accommodate extra lines of text. To enter a Tab character, press **Ctrl+Tab**.

- To select a row or column, click its control button along the left or top of the table. To select more than one row or column, drag across their control buttons. You can also select cell(s) first, then choose **Select** from the Table menu (**Table>Select** from the right-click menu), then either **Row** or **Column** from the submenu.

- To select all text (all rows and columns), choose **Select** from the Table menu (**Table>Select** from the right-click menu), then **All** from the submenu.

- To copy, paste and delete selected table text, use the **Copy**, **Paste** and **Delete** commands as you would for frame text. Alternatively, drag the bottom corner of a selected cell to copy its table text to any of the newly selected cells

- To format selected text, apply **character and paragraph properties** or **text styles** as with any text. Note that cell text with mixed formatting (for example, some bold and some plain) will revert to plain if you edit it via the Table context toolbar.

- Table text shares default properties with frame text. For details, see **Updating and saving defaults** on p. 65.

To change the table's structure and appearance:

- To adjust row or column size, drag the line separating control buttons. Note that you can adjust a row's height independent of the amount of text it contains.

- To delete one or more rows or columns, select them (or cell text) as described above, then choose **Delete** from the Table menu (**Table>Delete** from the right-click menu), then either **Row(s)** or **Column(s)** from the submenu.

- To insert new rows or columns, select one or more cells as described above, then choose **Insert** from the Table menu (**Table>Insert** from the right-click menu), then either **Rows...** or **Columns...** from the submenu. In the dialog, specify how many to add, and whether to add them before or after the selected cells.

- To merge cells into larger cells that span more than one row or column (for example, a column head), select a range of cells and choose **Merge Cells** from the Table menu (**Table>Merge Cells** from the right-click menu). The merged cell displays only the text originally visible in the top left selected cell. The original cells and their text are preserved, however—to restore them, select the merged cell and choose **Separate Cells** from the Table menu (**Table>Separate Cells** from the right-click menu).

- To copy cell contents (including text, formatting, borders, and colours) to a new cell in the same table, select the cell(s), press the Ctrl key and hover over the cell border(s) until the copy cursor is shown—click and drag the copied cell to its new cell location. To copy cell contents from one table to another table select the cells, right-click on a cell selection and choose **Copy**—select the area (of the same dimension) in the new table then select **Paste**.

- To move cell contents, select the cell(s), press the **Shift** key (instead of the **Ctrl** key) and hover over the cell border(s) until the move cursor is shown—click and drag the cell to its new cell location.

- **QuickFill** lets you fill a span of cells with the contents of an initially selected cell's contents. This one-to-many "replicating" operation is possible by dragging the bottom right-hand QuickFill handle of the initially selected cell outwards to encompass a contiguous block of cells either on the same row or column. Dragging diagonally will fill rows and columns simultaneously.

- To move cell contents within the same table, select the cells, and when the cursor is displayed, drag the cell(s) to the new location.

Using AutoFormat

To use style presets to customize the table's appearance:

- Choose **AutoFormat...** from the Table menu (**Table>AutoFormat...** from the right-click menu). The dialog presents a list of sample tables, which differ in their use of **Lines** (inner and outer cell borders), **Fill** (cell and table), **Font** (bold, italic, etc.), **Alignment** (left, centre, etc.) and **HTML editing** support.
- You can pick any sample and use the checkboxes to specify which of the sample's attribute(s) to apply to your actual table. This lets you "mix and match," for example by applying (in two passes) the Colour from one sample and the Font from another.
- To restore plain formatting, choose **[Default]**.

Setting Cell Properties

To customize the appearance of one or more cells "by hand":

1. Select the cell(s) and choose **Cell Properties...** from the Table menu.
   OR

   Table>Cell Properties... from the right-click menu.
   OR

   Cell Properties button on the Table context toolbar.
2. Use the dialog's **Border**, **Fill**, **Transparency**, **Margins** and **Orientation** tabs to apply cell formatting, then click **OK**.

Using the Border tab

To start, click to select one of the preset edge line configurations at the right. The Edge Selection box at the left shows exactly which lines (as indicated with bolding) will be applied to the table when you click **OK**. "Inside" line presets will affect inner border lines in the table, assuming you have more than one cell selected. Click the empty (lower-left) preset to remove all border lines.

Once you've chosen a preset you can customize the style of any or all lines in the configuration, first using the Edge Selection box to select which line(s) you want to edit, then clicking the **Line Style...** button to set line properties. Any lines indicated with arrows in the Edge Selection box will take on the new properties.

Formatting numbers

The Table context toolbar includes additional buttons, switched on with the **Spreadsheet functions** button, which let you vary how numbers are displayed. Number formats let you add commas and currency signs to numbers, express numbers as percents, control how many decimal places are displayed, etc. Number formats do not alter numbers internally—only the way numbers are displayed.

- Click the **Remove Formatting** button to remove any formatting.
- Click the **Currency** button to apply the currency format and symbol for your locale as suggested by Windows.
- Click the **Percent** button to convert a number to a percentage (multiply by 100 and append a percent sign).
- Click the **Comma** button to separate thousands by a comma and remove decimal places.
- Click the **Increase Decimal** or **Decrease Decimal** button to extend or reduce the number of decimal places shown.

For additional number formatting options:

- Click the **Custom Format** button.

The Custom Formatting dialog appears. Here you can select from any of the listed formats, construct custom formats (with colour for negative values, if you wish), and customize the list. The built-in list includes two currency symbol characters (one positive, one negative) for your locale, as supplied by Windows.

To apply a format to the current cell:

1. Select it in the list. The Sample box provides a preview of positive and negative values using the format.
2. Click **OK**.

To specify a custom format:

1. Type it into the box below the list, using any of the following symbols. (As you type the list automatically scrolls and highlights any matching entries.)

Display a digit if the number has one. If there are more digits in the number than #'s specified, then the extra digits left of the decimal place separator will be displayed.

0 Always displays a digit. If a number does not have a digit in this position then a zero (0) is displayed. If there are more digits in the number than 0's specified, then the extra digits left of the decimal place separator will be displayed.

- Display a negative symbol if the number is negative. No symbol is displayed if the number is positive.

+ Display a positive symbol if the number is positive, or a negative symbol if the number is negative.

(code) Display the formatted number in parentheses if the number is negative.

[colour] Display a negative number in the specified colour, e.g. Red. You can type any of these colour names: None, Black, White, Grey, Grey, Red, Green, Blue, Yellow, Orange, Cyan, Magenta, Burgundy, Dark Green, Mustard, Dark Blue, Purple, Sea Green
OR
You can enter colour values using one of these formats: RGB(xxx,yyy,zzz), CMYK(www,xxx,yyy,zzz), or HSL(xxx,yyy,zzz)

. Decimal separator

% Display numbers as percentages, e.g. 0.4 as 40% or 1.25 as 125%

/ Display decimal places as fractions, e.g. 0.4 as 2/5

0 Display no decimal places, e.g. 0.4 as 0. Same as entering 0.# (or having no format at all).

0.0 Display one decimal place, e.g. 0.4 as 0.4

0.00 Displays two decimal places, e.g. 0.4 as 0.40

0. Automatically calculate the number of decimal places to be displayed, e.g. 0.4 as 0.4

e Display number as an exponential (or scientific format), e.g. 0.4 as 4e-01. You can use the "0" character to specify the number of decimal places shown before or after the exponent, e.g. the value 123.456789 formatted as "+0.00 e+000" becomes "+1.23 e+002"; formatted as "+0.0000 e+00" it becomes "+1.2346 e+02".

WebPlus is not strict about the order in which the format codes are specified, and tries to interpret whatever you type.

2. To apply the custom format to the current cell (and save it in the list), click **OK**.

To delete a custom format:

- Select it and click the **Delete** button.

Inserting formulas

A table cell can display the result of a **formula** combining values of other cells with arithmetic operators and functions. Formulas are recalculated whenever values in the table change, so they're always up to date.

Any cell starting with the character "=" is treated as a formula. To enter or edit formulas, use the Table context toolbar's edit field. Note that you can only select or edit an entire formula, not just part of it.

Remember to enable the **Spreadsheet functions** button (on the Table context toolbar) to allow you to create formulas.

To display a cell's formula in the context toolbar's edit field:

- Click to select the cell containing the formula.

To enter a formula:

- Click the **Function** button on the Table context toolbar and choose a specific function from the drop-down menu.
  For example, if you start with a blank cell and choose **SUM()**, WebPlus adds "=SUM()" to the edit field and positions the text cursor between the brackets so that you can type numbers or cell references straight away.
  OR

- Click the **Function** button once to seed the edit field with an equal sign (or type "=" yourself), then continue to type the formula.

- Click the **Accept** button to update the selected cell.

See the WebPlus Help for a more information on formulas, their operators and functions.

Inserting a calendar

The **Calendar Wizard** helps you design a month-at-a-glance calendar to use in any site. You can create a postage-stamp graphic or a full-page "planner." Options include year, month, week and day labelling, room to write, and numerous style choices.

To insert a calendar:

1. Choose **Insert Calendar** from the Standard Objects toolbar's Table flyout.
2. Click again on your page (for a default sized calendar), or drag out to indicate the desired size of the calendar.

The **Calendar Wizard** then helps you pick a design and define options for your calendar.

Drawing Lines and Shapes

6

Drawing lines

WebPlus provides Freehand Line, Straight Line, Curved Line, and QuickShape tools for creating simple graphics. Using the **line tools** (found on a Standard Objects toolbar flyout), you can draw single lines, connect line segments together, or join line ends to **close** the line, creating a **shape** (see **Drawing shapes** on p. 112 for details). Use the Pointer tool and the Curve context toolbar to resize or reshape lines once you've drawn them.

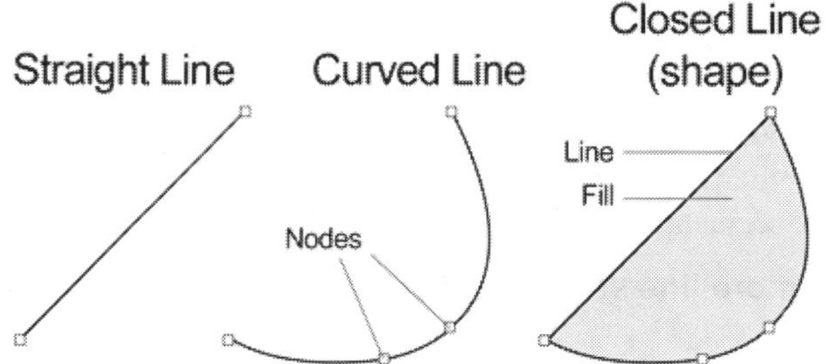

The **Freehand Line Tool** lets you sketch curved lines and shapes in a freeform way.

The **Straight Line Tool** is for drawing straight lines; rules at the top and/or bottom of the page; or horizontal lines to separate sections or highlight headlines.

The **Curved Line Tool** lets you join a series of curved or straight line segments using "connect the dots" mouse clicks.

To draw a freeform line (with the Freehand Line tool):

1. Click the Line Tools flyout on the Standard Objects toolbar and choose the **Freehand Line Tool**.
2. Click where you want the line to start, and hold the mouse button down as you draw. The line appears immediately.
3. To end the line, release the mouse button. The line will automatically smooth out using a minimal number of nodes.
4. To extend the line, position the cursor over one of its red end nodes. The cursor changes to include a plus symbol. Click on the node and drag to add a new line segment.

To draw a straight line (with the Straight Line tool):

1. Click the Line Tools flyout on the Standard Objects toolbar and choose the **Straight Line Tool** from the flyout.
2. Click where you want the line to start, and drag to the end point. The line appears immediately.

To constrain the angle of the straight line to 15 degree increments, hold down the **Shift** key down as you drag. (This is an easy way to make exactly vertical or horizontal lines.)

To extend the line, position the cursor over one of its red end nodes. The cursor changes to include a plus symbol. Click on the node and drag to add a new line segment.

To draw one or more line segments (with the Curved Line tool):

1. Click the Line Tools flyout on the Standard Objects toolbar and choose the **Curved Line tool** from the flyout. The Curve Creation toolbar appears, with three buttons that let you select which kind of segment you'll draw next.

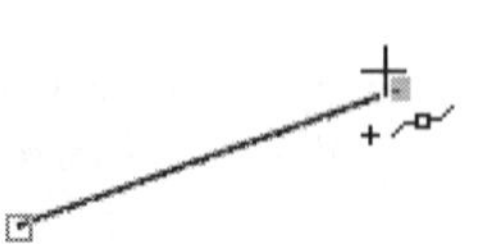

A **Straight** segment is simply a straight line connecting two nodes. (**Shortcut:** Press **1**)

A **Bézier** segment is curved, displaying control handles for precise adjustment. (**Shortcut:** Press **2**)

Smart segments appear without visible control handles, using automatic curve-fitting to connect each node. They are especially useful when tracing around curved objects and pictures. (**Shortcut:** Press **3**)

2. Select a segment type, then click where you want the line to start.

   - For a **Straight** segment, just click again (or drag) for a new node where you want the segment to end. **Shift**-click to align the segment at 15-degree intervals (useful for quick right-angle junctions).

   - For a **Bézier** segment, click again for a new node and drag out a **control handle** from it. (Control handles act like "magnets," pulling the curve into shape. The distance between handles determines the depth of the resulting curved line.) Click again where you want the segment to end, and a curved segment appears. Pressing the **Shift** key while you're drawing causes the new node's control handles to "snap" into orientation at 15-degree intervals with respect to the node. Normally, Bézier segments end in a symmetric (evenly rounded) corner, with control handles locked together. You can press **C** while drawing the segment to define a "cusp" or sharp corner.

   - For a **Smart** segment, click again for a new node. The segment appears as a smooth, best-fitting curve (without visible control handles) between the new node and the preceding node. Before releasing the mouse button, you can drag to "flex" the line as if bending a piece of wire. If the preceding corner node on the line is also smart, flexibility extends back to the preceding segment. You can **Shift**-click to create a new node that lines up at 15-degree intervals with the previous node.

3. To extend an existing line, repeat Step 2 for each new segment. Each segment can be of a different type.
   Note: To select the opposite end node of the curve (i.e., to extend the curve from the other end), press **Tab** before drawing the next segment.

4. To end the line, press **Esc**, double-click, or choose a different tool.

You can reshape the line after it's drawn (see below) or apply different weight, colour, or other attributes.

See WebPlus help for information on editing lines.

Drawing shapes

WebPlus provides Freehand Line, Straight Line, Curved Line, and QuickShape tools for creating simple graphics. **QuickShapes** are pre-designed objects that you can instantly add to your page, then adjust and vary using control handles. Another way of creating shapes is to **draw a line** (or series of line segments) and then connect its start and end nodes, creating a **closed shape**. Once you've drawn a shape, you can adjust its properties—for example, apply gradient or Bitmap fills (including your own bitmap pictures!) or apply transparency effects.

New shapes take the default line and fill (initially a black line with no fill).

You can easily turn shapes into Web **buttons** by adding **hyperlinks** or overlaying **hotspots**. The "Quick Button" QuickShape is especially intended for creating stylish button outlines!

QuickShapes

The QuickShape flyout contains a wide variety of commonly used shapes, including boxes, ovals, arrows, polygons and stars. You might use the **QuickShape** button for:

Decorative circles or polygons

Functional arrows, stars, callouts, and so on

Web buttons... any QuickShape will do, but try the unique **Quick Button** (circled at left) for a range of standard types. Add **hyperlinks** or **hotspots** to make your shapes "clickable"

A border framing your page, e.g. a box around the whole page.

Shaded panels, also known as screens, behind pictures to draw attention to them. The effect works equally well behind text.

To create a QuickShape:

1. Click the QuickShape button on the Tools toolbar and select a shape from the flyout. The button takes on the icon of the shape you selected.

2. Click on the page to create a new shape at a default size. Drag to adjust its dimensions.

3. When the shape is the right size, release the mouse button. Now you can alter the shape by dragging on its handles.

To draw a constrained shape (such as a circle):

- Hold down the **Shift** key as you drag.

All QuickShapes can be positioned, resized, rotated, and filled. What's more, you can adjust their designs using the Pointer tool. Each shape changes in a logical way to allow its exact appearance to be altered. The ability to alter the appearance of QuickShape objects makes them more flexible and convenient than clipart pictures with similar designs.

To adjust the appearance of a QuickShape:

1. Select it with the Pointer tool. One or more sliding handles appear next to the shape. Different QuickShapes have different handles.
2. To find out what each handle does for a particular shape, move the Node tool over the handle and read the HintLine.
3. To change the appearance of a QuickShape, drag its handles.

Closed shapes

As soon as you draw or select a line, you'll see the line's nodes appear. Nodes show the end points of each segment in the line. Freehand curves typically have many nodes; straight or curved line segments have only two. You can make a shape by extending a line back to its starting point.

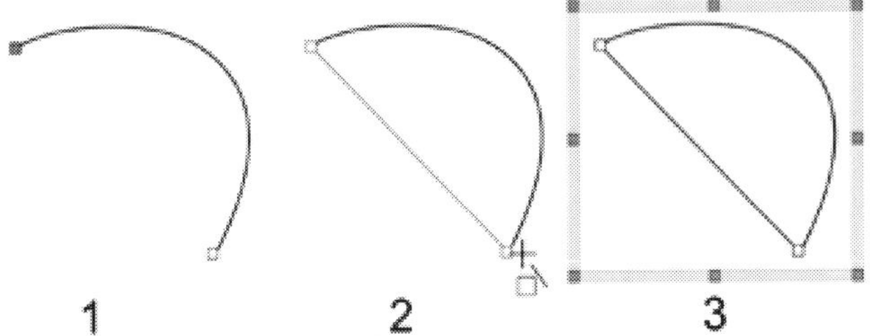

To turn a selected line into a shape:

- Select the line with the Pointer tool and click the **Close Curve** button on the Curve context toolbar.

You can go the other way, too—break open a shape in order to add one or more line segments.

To break open a line or shape:

1. With the Pointer tool, select the node where you want to break the shape.
2. Click the Break Curve button on the Curve context bar. A line will separate into two lines. A shape will become a line, with the selected node split into two nodes, one at each end of the new line.

You can now use the Pointer tool to reshape the line as needed.

See WebPlus help for information on editing shapes.

Working with Colour and Transparency

7

Applying solid colours

WebPlus offers a number of ways to apply solid colours to objects of different kinds:

- You can apply solid colours to an object's **line** or **fill**. As you might expect, QuickShapes and closed shapes have both line and fill properties, whereas straight and freehand lines have only a line property.
- Characters in text objects can have a colour, and text frames and table cells can have a background fill independent of the characters they contain.

You can use the Colour tab, Swatches tab or a dialog box to apply solid colours to an object.

To apply a solid colour via the Colour tab:

1. Select the object(s) or highlight a range of artistic text.
2. Click the **Colour** tab from which you can apply colour from one of several colour palettes.
3. Click the **Fill**, **Line**, or **Text** button at the top of the tab to determine where colour will be applied. The colour of the underline reflects the colour of your selected object.
4. Select a colour from the colour spectrum or sliders.

Use the **Colour Picker** on the Colour tab to select any colour already on your page, then apply it to another object. Hold down the mouse button to (magnify), then drag the cursor onto the desired colour and release.

To apply a solid colour via the Swatches tab:

1. Select the object(s) or highlight a range of artistic text.
2. Click the **Swatches** tab.
3. Click the **Fill**, **Line**, or **Text** button at the top of the tab to determine where colour will be applied.
4. Select a colour sample from the Publication palette (colours previously applied in your site) or Standard palette (supplied preset swatches).

Use **Format>Fill...** to apply colour via a dialog.

To change a solid colour's shade/tint (lightness):

1. Select the object and set the Line/Fill Swatch in the Colour tab so the Fill Swatch appears in front of the Line swatch.
2. From the Colour Display mode drop-down menu, select **Tinting**.
3. Drag the Shade/Tint slider to the left or right to darken or lighten your starting colour, respectively (the original colour is set at 0%). You can also enter a percentage value in the box (entering 0 or dragging the pointer back to its original position reverts to the original colour).

See WebPlus help for information on editing colours and managing gallery colours.

Using colour schemes

Each WebPlus site uses a global colour scheme which you can manage using the **Scheme Manager**. Each scheme has a name and consists of five complementary **basic colours** which you can apply to any design element. (These work like a paint-by-numbers system, as explained below.) In addition, each scheme includes **adjunct colours** which apply specifically to hyperlinks (default, followed and active) and page backgrounds. Switching to a different colour scheme instantly updates all elements that use scheme colours!

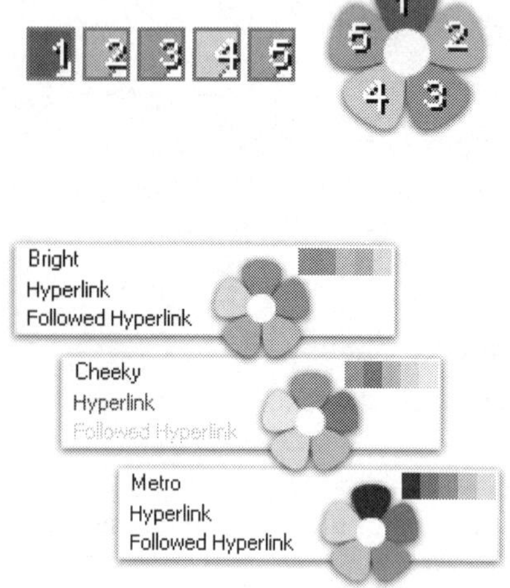

Colour schemes in WebPlus work much like a paint-by-numbers system, where various regions of a layout are coded with numbers, and a specific colour is assigned (by number) to each region (see the flower opposite, using the "Beacon" scheme). Swapping different colours into the "paint jars" numbered 1 to 5, while keeping the numbers on the flower the same, would automatically produce quite a different colouration.

In WebPlus, the "paint jars" are known as "Scheme Colour 1," "Scheme Colour 2," and so on. When you apply Scheme Colour 1 to an object, it's like saying, "Put the colour from jar number 1 here."

The example on the previous page shows how the scheme "Bright" could be applied to the site to replace the above "Beacon" scheme, the "Cheeky" scheme could then replace the "Bright" scheme, etc.

Each site can have just one colour scheme at a time; the current scheme is indicated in the Swatches tab. You can easily switch schemes, modify scheme colours, apply schemes to any site, even create your own custom schemes. Colour schemes are saved globally, so the full set of schemes is always available.

To select a colour scheme:

1. Display the **Swatches** tab. The five colours in the current scheme appear as numbered samples, from 1 to 5, at the bottom left-hand corner of the tab. (You'll also see additional samples labelled **H** (Hyperlink), **F** (Followed hyperlink), **A** (Active hyperlink) and **B** (Background), which apply to hyperlink and background page colours.)

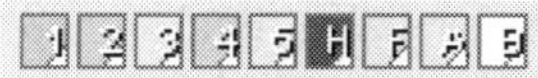

2. Click the **Colour Scheme** button on the default context toolbar (or choose **Tools>Scheme Manager...**) to display the **Scheme Manager**, which lists the various available schemes for your web site, each with a different set of five colours in the five "jars."
3. Select a different colour scheme sample from the list and click **OK**. Any regions in the site that have been assigned one of the five colour scheme numbers are updated with the corresponding colour from the new scheme.

You can repeat this selection process indefinitely. When you save a site, its current colour scheme is saved along with the document.

Adjunct colours

Besides the five basic colours, each scheme includes four **adjunct colours**.

- The **Hyperlink** colour (labelled **H**) applies to hyperlinked text **before** it's been clicked on.
- The **Followed Hyperlink** colour (labelled **F**), applies to hyperlinked text after a visitor has clicked to "follow" the link.
- The **Active Hyperlink** colour (labelled **A**), applies to hyperlinked text when a visitor's mouse button is depressed. Typically this is the colour shown after clicking and before the hyperlink's page is displayed.

- The page **Background** colour (labelled **B**) can be either a solid colour or picture. If you use a picture background with transparent regions, the Background colour is still active and will show through; otherwise the picture will cover the background colour.

The adjunct colours defined in the Scheme Manager normally apply throughout the site, with several important exceptions:

- Individual hyperlinks can specify their own colour. In the Hyperlinks dialog, uncheck **Use scheme hyperlink colours**. This will allow the underlying object's colour to show through on both the original and Followed hyperlink.

- Using the Master Page Manager (Background tab), you can override the Scheme Manager's Background colour/picture setting for a particular **master page**, which affects all pages that share that master page. **Pages** that don't use a master page default to the Scheme Manager setting, but you can override this via the Page Properties dialog (Background tab). In each case, uncheck **Use Scheme Manager settings** and set new options for **Page colour** and/or **Use picture**.

Applying scheme colours to objects

If you create new elements in a Web template site, or start a site from scratch, how can you extend a colour scheme to the new objects? Although you'll need to spend some time working out which colour combinations look best, the mechanics of the process are simple. Recalling the paint-by-numbers example above, all you need to do is assign one of the five scheme colour numbers to an object's line and/or fill.

To assign a scheme colour to an object:

1. Select the object and choose a **Fill**, **Line**, or **Text** button at the top of the Swatches tab depending on the desired effect.
2. From the bottom of the Swatches tab, click on a scheme colour (numbered 1 to 5) that you want to apply to the fill, line and text (or you can drag the colour instead).

If an object's fill uses a scheme colour, the corresponding sample will be highlighted whenever the object is selected.

Modifying and creating colour schemes

If you've tried various colour schemes but haven't found one that's quite right, you can modify any of the colours in an existing scheme and update the scheme, or create your own separately named scheme based on the existing scheme.

To modify a colour scheme:

1. Click the **Colour Scheme** button on the default context toolbar (or choose **Tools>Scheme Manager...**) to display the **Scheme Manager.**
2. Pick a colour scheme from the list on which to base your new scheme, and jump to the Edit tab at the top of the same dialog.
3. On the Edit tab, each of the five scheme colour numbers (plus the Hyperlink, Followed Hyperlink, Active Hyperlink and background Page colour) has its own drop-down list, showing available colours in the WebPlus palette.
4. To set or change a scheme colour or adjunct colour, simply click the adjacent button and select a new colour. Click **More Colours...** to display the Colour Selector.
5. To store the modified scheme in the Schemes Manager, click **Save Scheme...**. Leave the name unaltered to overwrite the existing scheme.
6. To apply the scheme to the current web site, click **OK**.

To create a new scheme, you can follow the above procedure but, at Step 4, enter a new scheme name instead of overwriting the existing scheme.

Setting transparency

Transparency effects are great for highlights, shading and shadows, and simulating "rendered" realism. They can make the critical difference between flat-looking illustrations and images with depth and snap.

Transparency may seem a bit tricky because by definition, you can't "see" it the way you can see a colour fill applied to an object. In fact, it's there all the time in WebPlus. Each new object has a transparency property: the default just happens to be "None"—that is, no transparency (opaque).

Transparencies work rather like fills that use "disappearing ink" instead of colour. The more transparency in a particular spot, the more "disappearing" takes place there, and the more the object(s) underneath show through. Just as a gradient fill can vary from light to dark, a transparency can vary from more to less, i.e. from clear to opaque, as in the illustration:

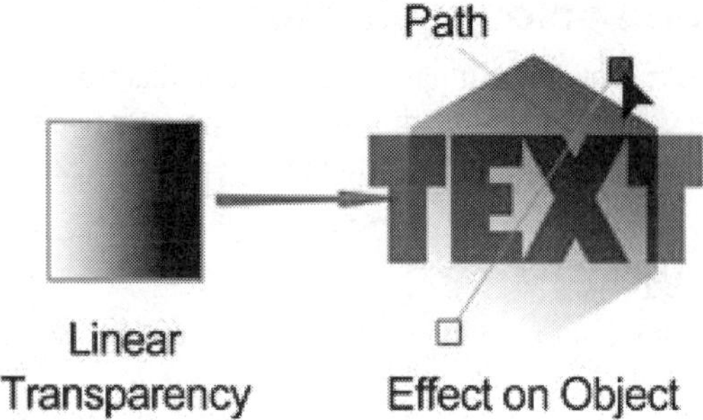

Here, the hexagonal shape has had a Linear transparency applied, with more transparency at the lower end of the path and less at the upper end. It makes a difference which object is in front (here, the pentagon); where there's more transparency, more of the object(s) behind will show through.

In WebPlus, transparency effects work very much like greyscale fills. Just like fills...

- Transparency effects are applied from the Studio—in this case, using the Transparency tab. (Transparency is also an option with the 3D Pattern Map filter effect.)
- The Transparency tab's gallery has thumbnails in shades of grey, where the lighter portions represent more transparency. To apply transparency, you click thumbnails or drag them onto objects.
- Most transparency effects have a path you can edit—in this case, with the **Transparency Tool**.

As for the effects available on the Transparency tab, all are comparable to the fills of the same name:

- **Solid** transparency distributes the transparency equally across the object.
- **Gradient** transparencies include linear, elliptical, and conical effects (each thumbnail's tooltip identifies its category), ranging from clear to opaque.
- The **Bitmap** gallery includes texture maps based on the Swatches tab's selection of bitmaps.

Applying transparency

There are two ways to apply transparency: using the Transparency tab or the Transparency tool.

To apply transparency with Transparency tab:

1. With your object selected, go to the Transparency tab.
2. For solid transparency, select the **Solid** button and pick a thumbnail from the solid transparency gallery. The lighter thumbnails represent more transparency (expressed as percentage Opacity).
   OR:

   For gradient transparency, choose the **Gradient** button and pick your thumbnail.
   OR:

   For Bitmap transparency, choose the **Bitmap** button and pick a thumbnail from a range of categories.
3. The transparency is applied to the object(s).

Alternatively, drag the desired thumbnail from the gallery to an object (the cursor changes to include a plus sign over suitable objects), and release the mouse button. The object takes the transparency and becomes the selected object.

To apply gradient transparency with Transparency Tool:

1. Select an object.
2. Click the **Transparency Tool** button on the Tools toolbar.
3. Click and drag on the object to define the transparency path. The object takes a simple Linear transparency, grading from 100% opacity to 0% opacity.

Editing transparency involves use of a dialog to let you add or subtract nodes from the gradient, apply different key colours to individual nodes, or vary the overall shading of the effect applied to the object.

See WebPlus help for information about editing transparency and managing gallery transparencies.

Images, Animation, and Multimedia

8

Importing images

WebPlus lets you insert images from a wide variety of file formats. Here's a quick overview:

- **Bitmapped** images, also known as **bitmaps** or **raster** images (e.g. GIF, JPG, PNG, etc.) , are built from a matrix of dots ("pixels"), rather like the squares on a sheet of graph paper. They may originate as digital camera photos or scanned images, or be created (or enhanced) with a "paint" program or photo editor.
- **Draw** graphics, also known as **vector** images, are resolution-independent and contain drawing commands such as "draw a line from A to B.".
- **Metafiles** are the native graphics format for Windows and combine raster and vector information.

You can also acquire images directly from **PhotoCDs** or via **TWAIN devices** (scanners or digital cameras).

Inserting pictures

There are several ways to bring an image into WebPlus. Decide in advance where you want to place the picture, and whether to insert it by embedding or by linking.

- **Detached** images float freely on a page, while **inline** images are incorporated with the text flow in a text object.
- **Embedded** images become part of the publication file, while **linking** places a reference copy of the image on the page and preserves a connection to the original file. Each approach has its pros and cons (see **Embedding vs. Linking** on p. 129.

To import an image from a file:

1. If you want to place the image inline, click for an insertion point in a text object. For a detached image, make sure text objects are deselected. To put the image in a frame, create the frame (see above) and select it.

2. In the main window:

   • Click the **Import Picture...** button on the Standard Objects toolbar's Picture flyout.
   • Choose **Picture...** from the Insert menu and select **From file...**.
   OR
   • Press **Ctrl+G**.
   OR

   • To replace an existing picture, select it and click the **Replace Picture** button on the Picture context toolbar.

   In WritePlus:
   • Choose **Picture File...** from the Insert menu.

3. Use the dialog to select the image file to open. Check **Preview** to examine images in the window at right.

4. If you check the **Place at native dpi** option and the image has a different internal setting, WebPlus will scale the image accordingly; otherwise it applies a screen resolution setting of **96 dpi**. Either way—or if you resize it downwards later on—the image retains all its original picture data until it's published.

5. Select either **Embed Picture** or **Link Picture**.

6. Click **Open**.

7. If there's a text insertion point in the main window, you'll be prompted whether to insert the image at the current cursor position. Click **Yes** if that's what you want.

If there was no insertion point (or you answer "No" to the insertion prompt), you'll see the mouse pointer change to the **Picture Paste** cursor. What you do next determines the initial size and placement of the detached image.

8. To insert the picture at a default size, simply click the mouse.
   OR
   To set the size of the inserted picture, drag out a region and release the mouse button.

Embedding vs. linking

Embedding means the image in WebPlus is now distinct from the original file. Embedding results in a larger WebPlus file, and if you need to alter an embedded image you'll need to re-import it after editing. Still, it's the best choice if file size isn't an issue and graphics are final.

Linking inserts a copy of the image file into the WebPlus project, linked to the actual file so that any changes you later make to it in the native application will be automatically reflected in WebPlus. Linking is one way of avoiding "bloat" by limiting the size of the publication file. On the other hand, you'll need to manage the externally linked files carefully, for example making sure to include them all if you move the WebPlus file to a different drive.

By default, WebPlus prompts you to embed pictures that are smaller than 256 KB, by pre-selecting the "Embed Picture" option in the Insert Picture dialog (but you can always select "Link Picture" instead). If you like, you can change the threshold file size or even switch off the automatic selection.

You can use the Resource Manager later on, to change an item's status from linked to embedded, or vice versa.

To pre-select embedding or linking based on file size:

1. Choose **Options...** from the Tools menu. You'll see the **General** tab.
2. To pre-select the "Embed Picture" option for images under a certain size, select the threshold size in the "Embed if smaller than" list. ("Link Picture" will be pre-selected for images larger than the threshold.)
3. To choose whether to embed or link each image, uncheck **Suggest embed/link picture**. You can still select either option in the import dialog; it will now remember and pre-select the last setting you used.

Setting picture export options

When you export your project as a Web site, WebPlus applies certain global settings to determine how each image—whether drawn, pasted in, or imported—ends up as a separate bitmap displayed on the Web page.

Here's a quick summary of initially defined conversion settings:

- Each referenced image is exported as a separate file.
- Any image you inserted as a GIF, JPEG, or PNG is exported as the original file, using its original file name.
- Inserted metafiles and all other graphics are regenerated as PNG images.

You can alter these settings, but before doing so you should review the "logic" WebPlus applies to publishing Web graphics. First, WebPlus has one **default format** to which all graphics will be converted on export—but you can make exceptions to this rule by specifying that certain image types should remain as their original file. Initially, PNG is the default format, but with **overrides** set for GIFs and JPEGs. That's why, using the initial settings above, GIFs and JPEGs stay as they are while all other graphics get converted to PNGs.

You can check and change these settings in the **Site Properties** dialog. The settings there are global and apply to all graphics in the site—but again you can make exceptions, in this case for individual graphics. To do so, you could either:

- Use the **Web Export Options** dialog or the **Web Export Manager** to set the export format of particular images on a case-by-case basis.
  OR
- Convert certain images to a specific format beforehand using the Tools>Convert to Picture.

This combination of global and local settings gives you almost total control (if you care to exercise it) over how your graphics make it onto your Web pages! Let's look first at how the global settings work.

To set global export options for Web graphics:

1. Choose **Site Properties...** from the File menu and select the Graphics tab. Then set options as follows:
2. Check **Optimize overlapping graphics** to have WebPlus analyze the site and (where a smaller file would result) output overlapping graphics as a single graphic. Whether this option makes sense will depend on your particular layout. Rather than use this global approach, you might consider using **Tools>Convert to Picture** in specific cases.
3. In the **Placed Graphics** section, to override conversion for images of certain formats (inserted JPEGs, GIFs, and/or PNGs), check which format(s) to preserve. Checking a format means that any image you've placed on a page using that format will stay in its original file format—exempt from conversion to the default format.

You can also use the Web Export Manager to set a local override, forcing WebPlus to export a particular image to a particular format.

4. Check **Remove spaces from original file names** if you want to revise graphic file names accordingly—useful if you find your Web server can't handle the spaces.
5. In the **Generated Graphics** section, select a preferred export format. This is the default format to which all graphics will be converted on export unless you set overrides.

Setting export options, title, and alternate text for individual graphics

The **Web Export Manager** is a Wizard that lets you set the export file format for individual graphics in the site, or for objects such as rotated text that will be converted to pictures on export. These local, picture-by-picture settings override the global settings (as set in **File>Site Properties**) which WebPlus uses to determine the export format. You can run the Wizard to check a single, selected picture; one or more specified pages; or the entire site. For each image, you can save it using different methods. Either:

- Choose a specific format (.JPG, .GIF, or .PNG) to export to (or just defer to site default settings). For JPGs, you can choose a level of compression. OR
- Save the file to a chosen path and file name on export. Perhaps you want to add more meaningful descriptive names to images on export (especially useful when maintaining your Web site) instead of having the images export with automatically generated image names.

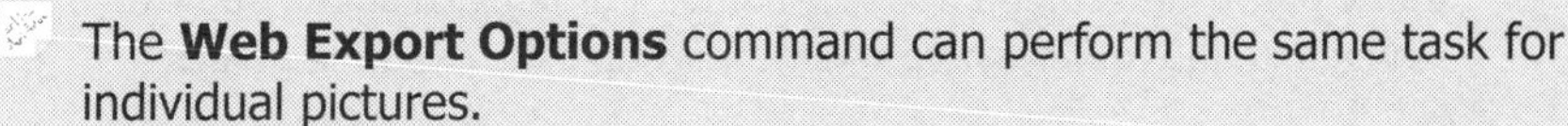
The **Web Export Options** command can perform the same task for individual pictures.

Let your own eye be the judge. Your best bet is to retain the **Use site default settings** option for all pictures to start with. Using the original global settings, this means that GIFs, JPEGs, and PNGs will be exported as their original files, while any others, including QuickShapes and closed shapes, will be published as PNGs. Then preview your site and determine if you want to vary the global settings or try a different output format for specific pictures.

Even if you don't change any format settings, you can set a picture **title** which will normally appear as a tooltip when the picture is moused over in a browser. You can also enter **alternate text** for Web site visitors to read while an image is downloading. Each such "tag line" you provide will appear inside the image frame during the time the image is being loaded into the visitor's Web browser. It's good practice to enter a concise, descriptive phrase describing each picture.

To set export format, title, and/or alternate text:

1. If you're checking just a single picture, you can select it first and choose **Web Export Options...** from the Format or right-click menu.
   OR
   To review Web export options for pictures throughout your site, choose **Web Export Manager...** from the Tools menu, or click the button on the Standard toolbar.

2. (Only if you're using the Export Manager) Select which objects or page(s) you want the Wizard to check, then click **Finish**. The Wizard cycles through graphics in the specified range, and displays each one in turn along with the Web Export Options dialog.

3. In the dialog's **Save Picture As** section, you can choose to either:

4. Save to a specific format with WebPlus choosing the name
   Enable the **Save in this format..** button. Click a GIF, JPEG, or PNG radio button and specify the export format for the current graphic. Otherwise, leave **Use site default settings** selected. If selecting JPEG, choose a compression quality from the Compression drop-down menu.
   OR

   Save to a specific format with WebPlus choosing the name
   Enable the **Save to my chosen path..** button and click the **Choose File...** button.
   The displayed dialog lets you export with the original image file name (enable **Use default name**) or choose a new image name (enable **Choose name** button and enter a new file name). For either method, you can navigate to the folder where you want to save the exported image.

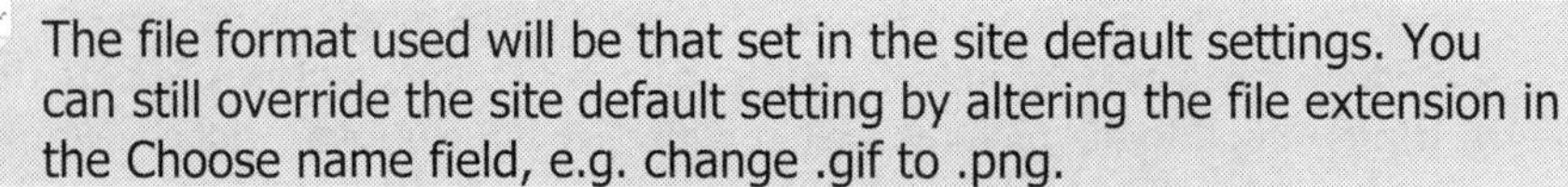

The file format used will be that set in the site default settings. You can still override the site default setting by altering the file extension in the Choose name field, e.g. change .gif to .png.

5. Check the **Exclude this picture from optimization..** option if you don't want the image to be combined into one exported image if overlapping with another image in your project.

6. (Optional) Choose from one of several resampling methods—WebPlus can resample when needed, the file will always be resampled or will never be resampled (original image will be used). Enable the appropriate radio button as needed. Changing the format will always resample.

7. To enter a title and/or alternate text for a graphic, type it in.

Applying image adjustments

The Picture context toolbar appears automatically when you select an image on the page. You can use the bar to improve the appearance of any image appearing in your drawing by adjusting **brightness** and **contrast** directly, setting levels and contrast automatically, fixing red eye or by applying **Image adjustments**. The context toolbar also hosts other photo manipulation tools.

Image adjustments are made possible with a comprehensive mix of colour correction/adjustment tools for use on your newly imported images. Levels, Colour Balance, Channel mixer, Dust and Scratch Remover and Hue/Saturation/Lightness corrective adjustments, amongst others, are available. Effect-inducing adjustments also range from the artistic Diffuse Glow to various blur effects. In fact, over 20 adjustments can be directly applied to your image not only individually but cumulatively.

Adjustments are managed in the **Image Adjustments** dialog. The gallery offers a one-stop shop for applying your adjustments—all supported by a dynamic preview window!

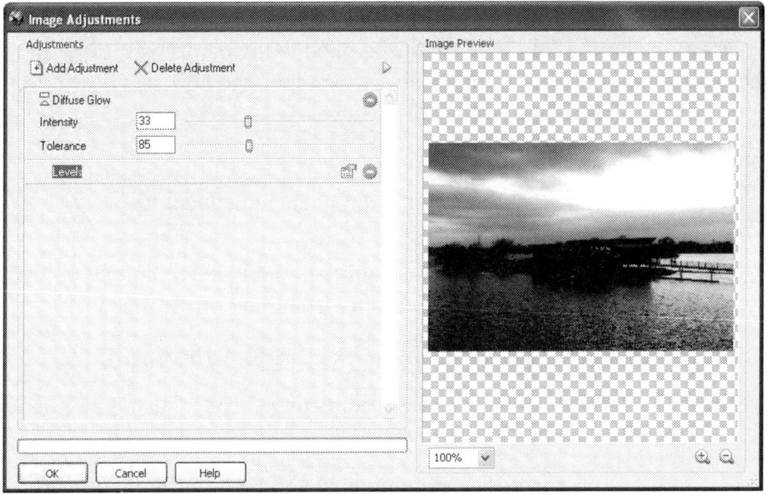

Adjustments can be applied to imported pictures as well as objects converted to pictures within WebPlus.

If you're looking to carry our some more advanced photo editing and have Serif's PhotoPlus software (10.0 or above) installed, you can use the **Edit in PhotoPlus** button on the Picture context toolbar to load the image directly into PhotoPlus. You can carry out your edit and save the file in PhotoPlus—if embedded or linked, the newly altered image is refreshed and updated in WebPlus automatically.

Adding an image adjustment

Adding an adjustment is as easy as choosing an option from a drop-down menu in the Image Adjustments dialog. To assist in the selection of an appropriate adjustment the list is separated into corrective adjustments (in the first half of the list), and effect-inducing adjustments (in the second half). As soon as an adjustment is selected it is added to a stack where additional adjustments can be added and built up cumulatively. Any adjustment can be switched on/off, deleted or reordered in this list. The order in which they appear in the stack may produce very different results—if you're not happy with your current order—WebPlus lets you drag and drop your adjustment into any position in the stack.

Adjustments are applied such that the most recently added adjustment always appears at the bottom of the list and is applied to the picture last (after the other adjustments above it). In the above example, the Diffuse Glow effect is applied to the picture first, followed by Levels.

To add an image adjustment:

1. Select the picture that you want to apply an adjustment to.
2. Click the Image Adjustments button on the Picture context toolbar.
   Choose **Picture>Image Adjustments** from the Format menu.
3. In the Image Adjustments dialog, click **Add Adjustment**.
4. From the drop-down list, select an adjustment. The adjustment is added to the scrollable window.
5. Select the adjustment. There are three methods to configure properties depending on the adjustment selected:

   Adjust settings by moving available sliders (if present) or use input boxes.
   OR
   For more complex adjustments, make changes in a pop-up dialog (click **Advanced Properties** to access).
6. Click the **OK** button.

 Some adjustments have no properties and are applied directly as they are selected.

Add more than one adjustment to the picture by repeating the above procedure.

To delete an image adjustment:

- With an adjustment selected, click the  button.

Switching on/off adjustments

In the same way in which a layer's contents can be made visible/invisible, the **Mute** button can be used to temporarily make an adjustment invisible or visible.

Modifying adjustments

The properties of any selected adjustment can be changed in one of two ways:

- Properties will be displayed alongside the adjustment appearing in the stack (in Image Adjustments dialog)—you can alter and experiment with these.
- The properties of an applied adjustment can be changed by clicking the **Advanced Properties** button alongside the effect (in Image Adjustments dialog)—this is because some effects are more complex to modify by their nature and need to be presented in a separate dialog.

Reordering adjustments

Adjustments can be moved around the stack to change the order in which they are applied to the picture. Drag an adjustment name to another position in the list while holding down the mouse button. A dark line indicates the new position in which the entry will be place if the mouse button is released.

Multiple adjustments

It's quite possible to apply several adjustments to the same image, and, depending on the order in which they are applied, to end up with a different final result.

Importing TWAIN images

If your scanner or digital camera provides **TWAIN** support, you can scan pictures directly into WebPlus using the TWAIN standard. Or, save the scanned image as a TIFF or PCX and then import into WebPlus.

To set up your TWAIN device for importing:

- See the documentation supplied with your scanner for operating instructions.

To import a scanned image:

- Choose **Picture...** from the Insert menu, then select **TWAIN** and **Acquire** from the submenu to open a file selection dialog.

If you have more than one TWAIN-compatible device installed, you may need to select which source you wish to scan with.

To select a different TWAIN source for scanning:

1. Choose **Picture...** from the Insert menu, then select **TWAIN** and **Select Source** from the submenu.
2. Identify the device you want to use as your TWAIN source.

Adding animation

WebPlus lets you add several varieties of eye-catching animation effects to any web page: **animated marquees**, **GIF animations**, and **Shockwave Flash** (.SWF) files. For any of the animation effects, you can preview the animation and/or customize the effect. Once placed into your Web site, the animations appear static, but they will spring to life once the site has been exported and a visitor views your page in a Web browser.

Bear in mind that animations do add to the "overhead" or load time your page requires, and may not display as quickly on the Web as when previewed in a Wizard.

Animated marquees

Animated marquees are an impressive way to add horizontally scrolling motion to a headline or catch phrase. You can choose the background colour, enter from one to three lines of text, define text properties (choose from any installed font), scroll direction, speed and alignment for each line. If you like, you can define any link destination type for the marquee (see **Adding hyperlinks and anchors** on p. 149). For the most compelling effect, select two lines with strongly contrasting text colours and opposing scroll directions.

Animated marquees appear as static graphics on the WebPlus page. You can cut, copy, move, and resize them just like other graphics. They will animate when **previewed** or viewed in a Web browser.

To create an animated marquee:

- Click the **Insert Animated Marquee** button on the Web Objects toolbar's Media flyout.
  OR
  Choose **Web Object** from the Insert menu and select **Animated Marquee...** from the submenu.

To edit an animated marquee you've already defined:

- Double-click the marquee. The Insert Animated Marquee dialog redisplays, with the current settings in place.

GIF animations

WebPlus lets you select and preview any animated GIF. They are particularly useful to illustrate particular themes or just add some fun to your page! All GIF animations appear as static images on the WebPlus page and, just like any image, you can cut, copy, move, and resize them just like other graphics. They will animate when **previewed** or viewed in a Web browser.

To preview and insert an animated GIF:

1. Click the **Insert Animated GIF** button on the Web Objects toolbar's Media flyout.
2. Use the dialog to select the image file to open. Check **Preview** to examine images in the window at right.
3. If you check the **Place at native dpi** option and the image has a different internal setting, WebPlus will scale the image accordingly; otherwise it applies a default screen resolution setting of **96 dpi**.

4. To keep the image separate from the WebPlus file (using a link to the source file) check **Link picture**. To include the image in the WebPlus project, check **Embed picture**.
5. Click **Open**.
6. You'll see the Picture Paste cursor. Click to insert the animation at a default size or drag to a custom size.

Flash files

A Flash (*.SWF) file is a viewable movie using the Flash™ Player format. (Flash is a vector-based program designed to create and display small files on the Web.) Flash files will play within your page view without the need for previewing in your browser (or WebPlus preview window). You can cut, copy, move, and resize them in lots of ways just like other graphics.

To see some Flash files in action, the **Gallery tab** hosts a stunning collection of Flash banners (each with pre-assigned Flash parameters already set).

To insert a Flash file:

1. Click the **Insert Flash file** button on the Web Objects toolbar's Media flyout.
2. Use the dialog to select the Flash file to open (click **Browse...** then select your .SWF file). To keep the animation separate from the WebPlus file (using a link to the source file) uncheck **Embed Flash file in site**.
3. In the Parameters window, click the **Add...** button to populate with parameter name/value pairs. A whole range of parameters can be added which can report values in the SWF file. Each parameter is appended to the list.
4. In the Additional Files window, build up a library of files (e.g., images) which are used to make up your Flash movie. Think of it as a local library in which supporting files are easily at hand and easily referenced. Click the **Add...** button to navigate to then select files for addition (use Ctrl-click or Shift-click for contiguous or on-contiguous file selection, respectively).
5. The Display box controls how the Flash movie is presented on your WebPlus page. Experiment with the options for different looping, transparency, alignment, scaling, and quality options then click **OK**.
6. You'll see the Picture Paste cursor. Click to insert the file at a default size or drag to set a custom size region.

To edit the Flash file:

- Select the Flash movie, right-click and choose **Edit Flash...**.

Adding sound and video

WebPlus lets you augment your Web pages with sound and video files in a variety of standard formats, including both **non-streaming** and **streaming** media. (Non-streaming files must download in entirety to a user's computer before they begin playing; streaming files require a special player that buffers incoming data and can start playing before the whole clip has arrived.)

There are actually two sound playback options—**background sound**, where a sound loads and plays automatically when a specific page is first displayed in the visitor's Web browser, and **linked sound**, triggered by a mouse click (for example on an icon or hyperlinked object). The supported audio formats are .AIFF, .AU, MIDI (.mid, .midi), .MP3, RealAudio (.ra, .ram), and .WAV.

Linked video works like linked sound. Supported video formats are .AVI, QuickTime (.mov, .qt), MPEG (.mpg, .mpeg, .mpe, .mpv), and RealVideo (.ram, .rv).

With both background and linked sound (or video), you have the option of **embedding** the source file in your project file, as opposed to keeping it separate. Although embedding any file adds to the size of the project, it is the default option because you'll no longer have to worry about juggling separate files or the chance of accidentally deleting one of them. When you publish your site, WebPlus takes care of exporting and copying both embedded and non-embedded files.

You won't be able to play back or edit sound or video files in WebPlus; you'll need to use an external media editor. Both types of files tend to take up a lot of space, more or less depending on the method of compression you've used. The large file size translates to long download times for non-streaming files. Media files also tend to be platform-specific: for example, there are different Windows, Mac, and Unix sound file formats. For these reasons, except for very short audio clips, one rarely encounters non-streaming media on the Web. However, if a fast connection is guaranteed, you can get away with using longer/larger non-streaming files. A technically complex alternative is to use streaming media such as RealAudio and RealVideo.

To add background sound to a page:

1. Right-click the page in the workspace and choose **Page Properties...**.
   OR
   Right-click the page entry in the Site tab's Site Structure tree and choose **Page Properties...** (or choose the item from the Edit menu).
2. From the Background tab, check **Use sound file**, then from the Open dialog, browse to the sound file you want to add. Once the file is selected, click **OK**.
3. If you do not wish to embed the file, uncheck the "Embed sound file in site" option.

If you choose not to embed your source files, we suggest you keep them together in a subfolder named "Media" or the like. When you publish your site, WebPlus exports and copies both embedded and non-embedded files into a common folder.

4. To have the sound play back as a continuous loop, check "Loop sound". Otherwise, it will play just once.
5. (Optional) Set **Export Options** to define an exported file name and physical location. (See **Setting picture export options** on p. 129).

The sound file will download and play back when the Web page displays in a browser.

With both linked sound and linked video, the basic question is how you want the visitor to be able to trigger the playback of a given media file. WebPlus offers the same basic options for both kinds of media:

- **From a hyperlinked object or hotspot:** You start with an existing object in the site, and **hyperlink** it to the media file, or use a **hotspot** over an image.
- **From an icon:** WebPlus provides an icon pre-linked to the media file. You then position the icon on your page.
- **From a picture:** You select an external picture file, which WebPlus then imports and links to the media file.
- **Inline:** A media "player" will be visible on your published Web page (rather than appearing after the user clicks a link, icon, or picture). In WebPlus, you'll see a marker on the page where the player will appear.

With the first option, the media file remains external and can't be embedded in your project. Options 2 to 4 give you the choice of embedding the media file.

To add linked sound or video to a page:

- To link from an object or hotspot, choose **Hyperlink...** from the Insert menu and select **A file on your hard disk** as the link target, then locate the media file.
  OR

To link from an icon, picture, or inline player:

1. Click the **Insert Sound Clip** or **Insert Video Clip** button on the Web Objects toolbar's Media flyout.
   OR
   Choose **Media** from the Insert menu and select either **Sound...** or **Video...** from the submenu.
2. Browse to locate the media file name.
3. Select a link display option (icon, inline, or picture).
4. If you do not wish to embed the file, uncheck the "Embed picture file in site" option.
5. Click **OK** to close the dialog, then click (or click and drag) with the cursor to place the icon, picture, or marker on your page.

Using the Photo Gallery

The simultaneous expansion of digital camera usage and Broadband services has created a fantastic opportunity for the publishing your photo collections on Web pages. There are a multitude of reasons for doing so but some common ones include:

- Hosting family photos for access by distant relatives
- Special occasions (parties, Christmas, holidays)
- Cataloguing collections (e.g., of animals)

A great Photo Gallery feature is the ability to adopt different gallery types—choose Thumbnail Grid, Thumbnail Strips/Bars or even Full Images with theme navigation arrows. The example below shows the "Thumbnail Strip (Top)" type which is ideal for viewing and navigating images quickly. Thumbnail Strips and Bars offer theme navigation arrows whereas Thumbnail Grids display full-size images on thumbnail click.

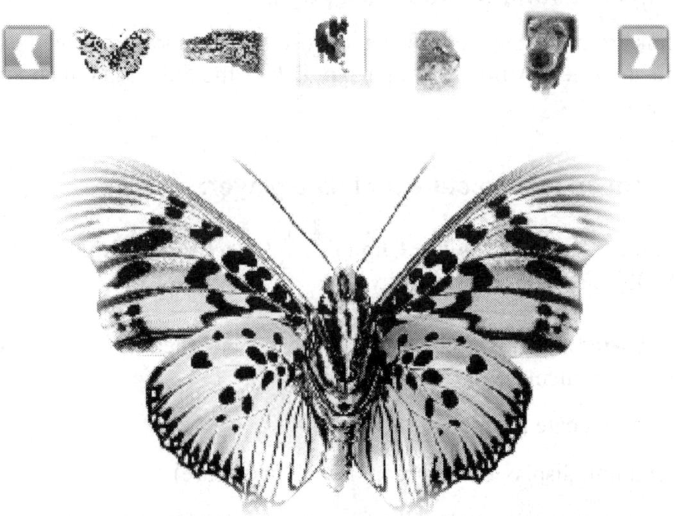

Photos can be imported by file or folder, or from a TWAIN device (digital camera/scanner). Once arranged in a gallery structure the photo's thumbnails can be manipulated in a variety of ways. It's possible to:

- Reorder by drag and drop, or using arrangement buttons.
- Sort in specific order.
- Rotate (in 90° anti-clockwise increments)*.
- Temporarily expand thumbnail size for review.
- Add captions.
- Apply decorative frames (from gallery).
- Apply effects such as drop shadows, glows, bevels or a custom Filter Effect.
- Apply image adjustments.

*Automatic rotation of digital camera images (landscape to portrait) is possible (if supported by camera).

For the web visitor, the gallery displayed will offer navigable theme arrows which can jump to next/previous thumbnails (with single-click) or scroll through thumbnails (by holding the mouse button down).

Creating the Gallery

The Photo Gallery is inserted on the page, just like an individual image, after collecting your images together from file, folder, camera, or scanner.

All the images are output as JPGs regardless of the original image type and the settings in **File>Site Properties>Graphics**.

To insert a Photo Gallery:

1. Click the **Insert Photo Gallery** button on the Standard Objects toolbar's Picture flyout.
   OR
   Select **Photo Gallery...** from the Insert menu.
2. From the dialog's Photos tab, choose whether to:
   - Click the **Add Files** button to navigate to then select the image file(s) to open. Use Ctrl-click or Shift-click to select multiple non-contiguous or contiguous files. Use the **Preview** window to examine the selected images.

     Choose whether to check the **Place at native dpi** option (the image's original resolution) or check **Place at 96 dpi** (to apply a screen resolution setting of **96 dpi**). Click **Open**.
     OR
   - Click the **Add Folders** button to navigate to a folder then add a selected folder containing your images.
     OR
   - Click the **Add TWAIN** button to acquire images form a digital camera or scanner. If needed, select your TWAIN source in advance of the Acquire process. Use **Acquire...** and **Select Source...** from the drop-down menu.
   - To delete a thumbnail, select it and click the **Delete** button.

Avoid inserting large image files unnecessarily, e.g. if acquired directly from digital cameras set for high-resolution (2400 x 1800). If you own Serif PhotoPlus you can reduce all image sizes in bulk (with a macro) before inserting them. Alternatively, use another photo editor to resize manually.

3. Optionally, select one or more gallery thumbnail for manipulation, i.e.

   - Reorder the thumbnails by drag and drop.
     OR

     Use the **Move Up**, **Move Down**, **Move to Start** and **Move to End** buttons in the Arrangement box).

   - Rotate in 90° intervals anti-clockwise with multiple clicks of the **Rotate** button.

   - Add a caption under the image with the **Caption** button (captions only show during preview or on live site).

   - Use the **Sort** button's drop-down menu to sort all images by filename (default), file size, date taken, or picture dimensions.

   - From the Effects box, apply different Frame styles, **effects** or **image adjustments**. Each drop-down menu offers commonly used options, along with a more advanced **Custom...** option (effects and adjustments only). Check **Apply To All** to alter every gallery image; uncheck to affect only selected images.

4. Jump to the Settings tab in the same dialog, and select a **Gallery type** from the drop-down menu. Each type offers a different style for presenting your images—try each one out until you find one you like in the accompanying Preview window.

5. (Optional) Choose an alternative accompanying theme arrow. These are based on theme graphics so the style can be easily swapped (see **Incorporating theme graphics** on p. 49). The gallery preview is updated to reflect the new arrow design.

6. Click the **Finish** button.

7. To insert the gallery at a default size, position the displayed cursor where you want the gallery to appear on the page, then simply click the mouse.
   OR
   To set the size of the inserted gallery, drag out a region and release the mouse button.

Editing the Photo Gallery

Once added to the web page the Photo Gallery can be edited. Updating images, changing gallery types, reorganizing and applying different set of effects are all possible.

To edit a Photo Gallery:

1. Select a gallery already present on your web page.
2. Double-click the gallery.
   OR
   Right-click the gallery and choose **Edit Photo Gallery...**.

The Insert Photo Gallery dialog is displayed. The options available are the same as those available when the gallery was created.

Once a gallery is placed on the page it's also possible to change the gallery thumbnail size, horizontal/vertical spacing (gap between thumbnails), and the border size around the gallery by dragging the square control handles, i.e.

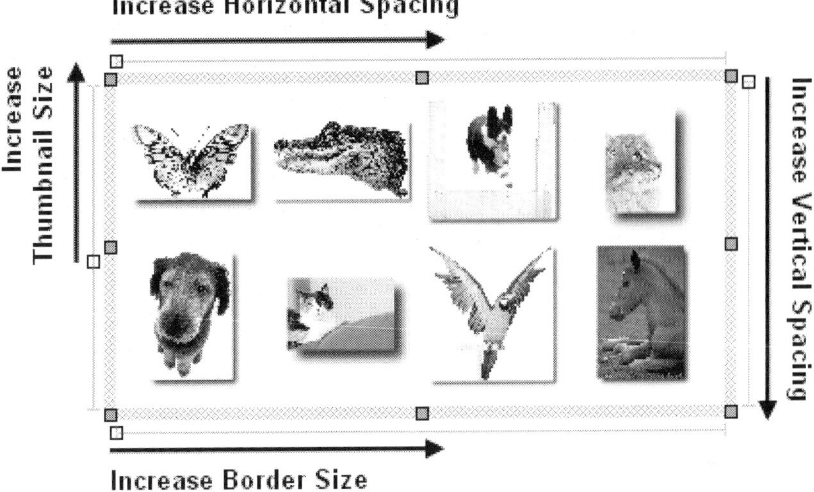

To decrease values (not illustrated) simply drag the control handle in the opposite direction. You may notice that the Photo Gallery context toolbar, displayed when you select any gallery, also allows you to edit these values—alter the **Size** (of thumbnail), **Spacing (H)** for horizontal spacing, **Spacing (V)** for vertical spacing and a **Border Size** (all in pixels). Enter an absolute value (in pixels) in the input box, click the up/down arrows or use the sliders on each option's right arrow button.

Linking remote images

It is possible to connect to any image currently available on the Internet. However, to prevent copyright infringement it's advisable to use images from a reliable image hosting service. Many exist on the Internet but services such as **ImageShack** (http://www.imageshack.us/) are particularly popular. Of course you may be able to link to other images (from a friend or colleague's web site) where legal implications are not as relevant. Either way, you can enhance the visual appeal of your web site by adopting third-party images, leaving you to concentrate on other areas of design or content generation.

To insert a remote image:

1. Go to **Insert>Picture>Remote link...**.
2. In the dialog, enter the absolute URL for the image.
3. Click **OK**.
4. You'll see the mouse pointer change to the Picture Paste cursor. What you do next determines the initial size and placement of the image.

   To insert the image at a default size, simply click the mouse.
   OR

   To set the size of the inserted image, drag out a region and release the mouse button.

Hyperlinks and Interactivity

9

Adding hyperlinks and anchors

Hyperlinking an object such as a box, some text, or a picture means that a visitor to your Web site can click on the object to trigger an event. The event is most commonly a jump to one of the following:

- a Web page (either on your site or somewhere else on the Web)
- an e-mail composition window
- a graphic, text, audio, or video file on you hard disk
- to an anchor (a designated target within a Web page)
- a full-size image view of any image
- a shopping cart
- navigation element
- user data

Well-designed hyperlinks are an important aspect of **site structure**. They help visitors navigate through your site and serve as an important adjunct to logical page relationships as shown in the Site Structure tree. (But don't overlook the time-saving advantages of using theme graphics for **navigation elements** such as navbars and Previous/Next buttons.)

To add a hyperlink:

1. Use the Pointer tool to select the single or grouped object or highlight the region of text to be hyperlinked.

You can also simply click for an insertion point in text. If you select in—or immediately before/after—a word, then the whole word will be hyperlinked. If your selection point has a space on both sides, WebPlus inserts helpful text (for example, the name of the target page).

2. Click the **Hyperlink** button on the Tools toolbar.
   OR
   Choose **Hyperlink...** from the Insert menu or the object's right-click menu.

   The Hyperlinks dialog appears.

3. Click to select the link destination type, and enter the specific hyperlink target.

4. Depending on the link type, choose type-specific options, the Target window or frame, and Other properties such as Title name and a shortcut access key.
   Note: As a visual cue, hyperlinked words are normally underlined and appear in the colour you've specified for Hyperlinks in the Scheme Manager or elsewhere (see **Using colour schemes** on p. 118).

5. Click **OK**.

To modify or remove a hyperlink:

1. Use the Pointer tool to select the object, or click for an insertion point inside the linked text. (It's not necessary to drag over a hyperlinked region of text.)

2. Click the **Hyperlink** button on the Tools toolbar's Hyperlinks flyout.
   Choose **Hyperlink...** from the Insert or right-click menu.

The Hyperlinks dialog appears with the current link target shown. If the link is in text, the whole text link highlights.

- To modify the hyperlink, select a new link destination type, target, and/or options.
- To remove the hyperlink, click the **No Hyperlink** button.

Inserting an anchor

An **anchor** is a specific location on a page that can serve as the target for a hyperlink. Invisible to the Web page visitor, it typically marks a point within some text (such as the start of a particular section) or an image at some point down the page. Anchors are useful if your page has enough content to be divided into sections, but not enough to require carving up into separate pages. These let the reader jump to related content without leaving the current page. In the same way, keeping Web visitors on the same page makes it less likely they'll get "lost' while perusing the information on your site.

To insert an anchor:

1. Use the Pointer tool to select the target object, or click for an insertion point inside the target text.
2. Click the **Anchor** button on the Tools toolbar's Hyperlinks flyout.
3. In the dialog, type a name for the anchor and click **OK**.

To edit an existing anchor:

- Use the **Anchor Manager** on the Tools menu to view, rename, or remove an anchor attached to a particular object.

Adding hotspots to a page

A hotspot is a transparent hyperlink region on a Web page. Usually placed on top of graphics, hotspots act like "buttons" that respond when clicked in a Web browser. They are especially useful if you want the visitor to be able to click on different parts of a picture (such as a graphic "menu" or map of your site). You can draw and edit hotspots by hand, or create them to match an existing shape.

To draw a hotspot:

1. Click the **Insert Hotspot** button on the Tools toolbar's Web Objects flyout.
2. Click and drag to draw a rectangular hotspot region. The Hyperlinks dialog appears.
3. Click to select the link destination type, and enter the specific hyperlink target (see **Adding hyperlinks and anchors** on p. 149).
4. Click **OK**.

To match a hotspot to an existing shape:

1. Draw the hotspot as described above, and create the shape as described in **Drawing shapes** on p. 112.
2. Select both objects and choose **Fit Hotspot to Shape** from the Tools menu.

The two objects will still be separate, so you can easily delete the shape if it's no longer needed once you've used it as a template to produce a hotspot of a desired shape.

To modify a hotspot hyperlink:

- Using the Pointer tool, double-click the hotspot.
  OR
- Click to select the hotspot and click the **Hyperlink** button on the Tools toolbar (or choose **Hyperlink...** from the Insert menu).

The Hyperlinks dialog appears with the current hotspot link target shown.

- To modify the hyperlink, select a new link destination type and/or target.
- To remove the hyperlink, change the link destination to **No Hyperlink**.

Editing hotspots

You can move and resize hotspots on the page, just like other objects. A selected hotspot has both an outer bounding box and an inner outline, which serve different purposes.

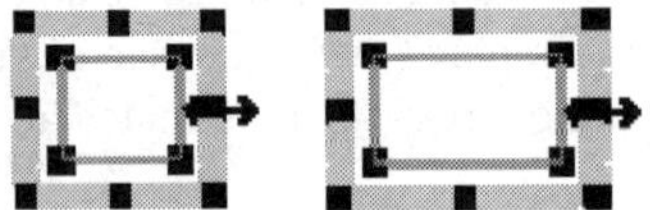

To move or resize a hotspot:

- Click to select the hotspot, then:
    - To move, click and drag from the centre, or from the hotspot's bounding box. To constrain the hotspot to vertical or horizontal movement, hold down the **Shift** key while dragging.
    - To resize, click and drag on its outer (bounding box) handles.

By editing the inner outline, you can convert rectangular hotspots into freeform shapes that closely match the parts of the underlying graphic you want to be "hot." To edit the outline, first move the mouse pointer over the hotspot's inner outline until the cursor changes to indicate whether you're over a node or a line.

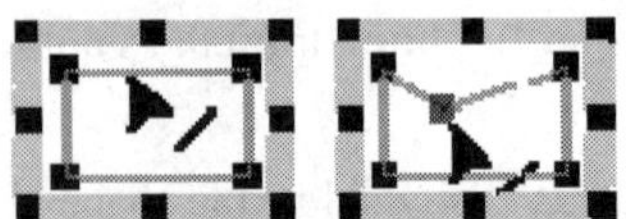

To create an extra node on a hotspot:

- Click anywhere along the hotspot's outline when you see the cursor.

To change the shape of a hotspot's outline:

- Click and drag a node when you see the cursor.

Adding rollovers

The term **rollover** refers to an interaction between a mouse and a screen object. For example, you can point your mouse at a graphic (such as a navigation bar button) on a Web page, and see it instantly change colour or become a different picture. When you point to a Web page object, your mouse pointer physically enters the screen region occupied by the object. This triggers an event called a "mouseover" and, if the underlying code is there to "trap" this event, it can trigger some other event—such as swapping another image into the same location. An object whose appearance changes through image-swapping in response to mouse events is called a **rollover graphic**.

As a prerequisite to creating a rollover graphic in WebPlus, you'll need to prepare a picture for each distinct rollover state, using a separate graphics program. The necessary event-trapping code is generated for you automatically. WebPlus also lets you directly import rollover graphics created in Serif DrawPlus.

Rollover options

Adding rollovers is basically a matter of deciding which rollover state(s) you'll want to define for a layered graphic, then specifying an image for each state. DrawPlus provides four basic choices:

- **Normal** is the "resting" state of the graphic before any rollover, and is always defined.

- **Over** is the state triggered by a mouseover— when the mouse pointer is directly over the object. For example, a button's text might change colour, or an outline appear, to show the button is "alive." Prior to a mouse click (see Down), moving the pointer in and out of the graphic's area will alternate between Over and Normal.

- **Down** is triggered by a mousedown on the graphic. The term derives from a typical button's behaviour: its "up" state changes to "down" once it's been clicked.

It takes more than a mousedown to trigger the button's hyperlink—it takes a complete click, i.e. a mousedown and a following mouseup event, both of them <u>on the button</u>. If the user has moved the mouse out of the button region before the mouseup, and you haven't defined Down+Over (see below), the button can appear to get "stuck" in the Down state.

- **Down+Over** (only available if Down is activated) implies a mouseover that occurs when the graphic is already Down, i.e. after it's been clicked. If you don't activate Down+Over, then the button just stays in its Down state after a mousedown event, which can cause unresponsiveness (see the above Note). For a more responsive button, set the Normal and Down states to graphic A, and the Over and Down+Over states to graphic B. In this case the Down state effectively means "Down+Not Over" and the button will revert to its Normal appearance if the user moves the mouse outside the button, even after a mousedown. It sounds complex, but it works!

You'll also have the option of specifying a **hyperlink** event—for example, a jump to a targeted Web page—that will trigger if the user clicks on the object. And you can even group buttons on a page so they work together and only one at a time can be down.

To create a rollover graphic:

1. In a suitable image-editing program, create the variant source images for each state you'll be defining. (See **Creating variant source images** on p. 155.)
2. Click the **Insert Rollover** button on the Web Objects toolbar's Insert flyout.
   OR
   Choose **Web Object** from the Insert menu and select **Rollover...** from the submenu.
3. Specify which rollover states (see above) you want to activate for each graphic by checking boxes in the Rollover Graphic dialog. For each one, use the **Browse** button to locate the corresponding source image and specify Export Options for that image (see **Setting picture export options** on p. 129).
4. Check **Embed files in site** if you want to incorporate the image(s) in the WebPlus file. (For details, see **Embedding vs. linking** on p. 129).
5. Check either **Normal** or **Down** as the button's initial rollover state.
   For example, common sense dictates that on a site's actual Home page you should initially show the "Home" button itself as down, and/or unresponsive to mouse actions—after all, the viewer is already on that page—whereas buttons that link to other pages should be in their normal "up" state and responsive.
6. Click **Set...** to define a hyperlink target for the button. (For details, see **Adding hyperlinks and anchors** on p. 149).

7. Check **Radio button** if you want to link all the buttons (on a given page) that have this option checked, so that only one of them at a time can be down.
   If you use this technique, make sure all rollover graphics you want to link have the option checked. Although it doesn't matter how the buttons are distributed on the page, typically they'll constitute a visible unit like a navigation bar. Any buttons with the option unchecked are independent.
8. Click **OK**. The first time you define a rollover state, you'll see rollover layers established in the document (see below).

WebPlus displays the image assigned to the Normal state. It's a good idea to **preview the page** and test each rollover object, then return to WebPlus and revise as needed. When you preview or publish the Web site, WebPlus takes care of exporting one image file for each rollover state, and the HTML file for the published page incorporates the JavaScript code for the rollover event trapping.

To revise a rollover graphic:

1. Right-click the graphic and choose **Edit Rollover...**.
2. Make new selections as needed and click **OK**.

Creating variant source images

For each object with at least one activated rollover state, you'll need to provide a source image. It's the often subtle differences between the Normal image and the "variants" that make the object appear to switch from one state to another. For example, if you've checked the "Over" state for an object, you need to include a variant image that the Web page can display when the button is moused over. In the following example, two variants of a Home button are shown—one showing the button highlighted (on mouse over), and a second image in its default Normal state.

You'll need to create these source images in a separate image-editing program.

Here are some things to consider:

- Variant images will stretch to fit into the region occupied by the Normal image, so all the source images should have the same dimensions.
- Make sure the variants are all in precise registration with the Normal image, so there's no unintended movement when images are swapped on rollover. To simplify matters, use an image editor with layering capability and create each variant on a separate layer directly above the Normal image.
- WebPlus displays only the Normal image, so preview the effect of swapping graphics by hiding and showing layers in the image editor.
- You only need to provide variant source images for the rollover states you've activated.
- Once you're satisfied with the source images, export each layer to a separate file, and then return to WebPlus to define the rollovers.
- When assigning the source images, you'll need to choose between linking and embedding. As long as a source image is linked (not embedded), WebPlus will always use the latest version of a file. So as a rule, until you're truly sure your source images are final, you may wish to uncheck the "Embed files" box so that linked images will be used. You can easily repeat the assignment process, using embedding instead, once the source images are final. If you do find yourself needing to update an image that's already been embedded, the best way is to save the revised file under a different name, then repeat the assignment process and specify the new file instead of the old.

Importing DrawPlus rollovers

Serif DrawPlus provides not only advanced image editing and layering capabilities, but built-in tools for producing rollover graphics. For example, you can preview just a region of your screen in a Web browser, and set export options. DrawPlus outputs of a series of image files (for example, MYFILE_01.GIF, MYFILE_02.GIF, etc.) with variants for each rollover state, and a single HTML file (for example, MYFILE.HTML) that includes the JavaScript code.

To import a DrawPlus rollover graphic:

1. Choose **Web Object** from the Insert menu and select **DrawPlus Rollover...** from the submenu.
2. Locate the HTML file for the rollover graphic. Keep **Embed graphic files** checked to incorporate the images into the project, or uncheck to link them.
3. Click **OK**.

WebPlus automatically inserts a placeholder for the object.

Adding navigation elements

In WebPlus, certain types of **theme graphic** called **navigation elements** are programmed to understand your site structure, making it easy to design a site that's simple to navigate. You just select a navigation element—such as a **Navbar** (navigation bar), or a **Previous** or **Next** button—from the Studio's Theme Graphics tab (or a dialog) and WebPlus does the rest!

Previous/Next buttons automatically link laterally, to adjacent pages on the same level. Navbars combine buttons with popup menus to facilitate movement between the various sections and levels of a site. For example, in this navbar the buttons provide links to the Home page and various top-level section pages, while popup menus link to child pages within each section.

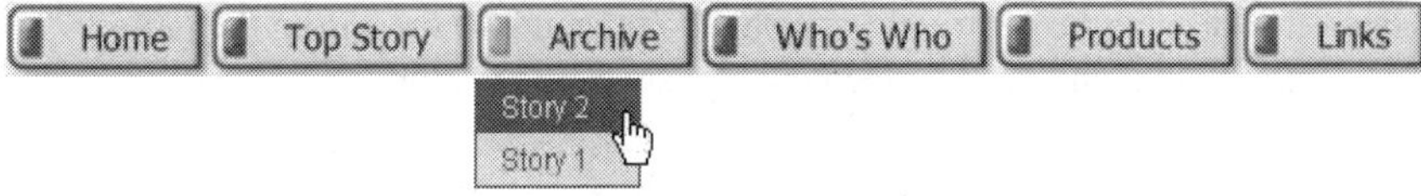

You can easily install navigation elements at any level of your site, reconfigure them to link to a particular part of the site, change the appearance of the popup menu, and exclude particular pages from navigation as needed.

When you define a navigation element, you use standard terminology like "Parent Level" or "Previous/Next" to specify which part of the site should be linked to, relative to the starting page—i.e. which buttons should be included.

Because navigation elements "understand" your site structure, they update dynamically if you alter page names or relationships, or cut/paste the navigation element to another page! The links are always relative to the page where the element is located. For example, if a navbar links to child-level pages, it will continue to do so—even if that means linking to different pages—if you move it, or the page it's on, to a different place in the structure.

You can place navigation elements on **master pages**, too—which saves you the trouble of pasting the same element to multiple pages. A navigation element on a master page behaves as if it's on each page—consistent with the notion that its buttons and menus are relative to where each page sits in the overall site structure.

You can make use of **tokens** (see p. 172) to add variables to your navigation—use for breadcrumb navigation that will update dynamically if you add, remove or change pages within the site.

To add a navigation element:

1. Display the Studio's **Theme Graphics tab**.
2. In the Categories tree, select a category to browse.
   Click **Current Site** to view theme graphics already in use, for example if you want to add an element again.
   OR
   Expand the **Sets** or **Types** list, and then select a category to view its gallery.
   OR
   With "Theme Graphics" selected as a category, click the **Current Site**, **View Sets**, or **View Types** thumbnail in the lower Theme Graphics section. Then click the thumbnail for the type or set you want to browse.

Browse the gallery of available elements and click a particular theme graphic to add it at the centre of your page. You can also drag from the gallery thumbnail and drop an element at a specific location.
OR

1. (To add a navigation bar) Click the **Insert Navigation Bar** button on the Web Objects toolbar's Insert flyout, or choose **Navigation Bar...** from the Insert menu.
2. On the dialog's **Theme Set** tab, choose a Horizontal or Vertical orientation and select a theme for the navbar.
3. Customize the **Navigation Type** and **Popup Menu Properties** as described in steps 2 and 3 below (for reconfiguring a navbar).
4. Click **OK**.

Because navigation elements are theme graphics, you can use the Theme Graphics tab to select coordinated design elements (buttons, etc.) for a consistent look, and change the overall appearance with a single click. To edit theme graphic properties such as font, text colour, and mouseover fill colour, select the object and click its [T] **Edit** button. (You can also right-click it and choose **Edit Theme Graphic....**) For details, see **Incorporating theme graphics** on p. 49.

Navigation bars have their own dialog for reconfiguring navigation properties.

To reconfigure a navigation bar:

1. Double-click it, or right-click it and choose **Edit Navigation Bar....**
2. On the dialog's **Navigation Type** tab:
   - Select which buttons should be included in the navbar: Top Level, Parent Level, Same Level, Child Level, Home, Previous and Next, Previous, Next, or Up. (See the diagram and discussion above.)
   - Depending on the main selection, you can opt to include the **parent page** and/or the **Home page**.
   - As a design choice, you may elect to **Make all buttons the same size** (otherwise buttons will autofit to their text) and/or **Use page names** (otherwise buttons will have functional names like "Previous" or "Home").
3. On the dialog's **Popup Menu Properties** tab:
   - To prevent the popup menu from appearing, uncheck **This navigation object has menus**.
   - To change settings for the text and appearance of the popup menu, use the controls at the right.

By default, all pages in the tree are **included in navigation**—that is, they can be linked to by navigation elements. You can **exclude** certain pages (any but the Home page) so they'll be ignored by navigation elements. For example, suppose you had a section of reference or archival pages that you didn't want visitors to explore top-down. Excluding the parent page for that section would remove it from the navbar. Note that excluding the page from navigation doesn't remove it from the site—the page will still appear in the Site Structure tree and you can still install **hyperlinks** to it; it just won't show up in a navbar.

Included pages show a ✔ mark in their page entry in the Site tab's Site Structure tree, while excluded pages lack the mark.

To exclude a page from navigation:

- On the Studio's **Site** tab, right-click the page in the Site Structure tree and choose **Page Properties...**. Below the tree, uncheck **Include in Navigation.**

The setting is also available in the Page Properties dialog (Page tab).

If you're looking to rearrange the order or hierarchy of your navigation bar items to be different from you Site Structure, WebPlus will allow you to customize any navigation bars—you can also add, edit, or delete elements which will access a range of link destination types (see **Adding hyperlinks and anchors** on p. 149) just as in Site tab's Site Structure.

To customize a navigation bar:

1. Double-click the navigation bar.
   OR
   Click the **Insert Navigation Bar** button on the Web Objects toolbar's Insert flyout, or choose **Navigation Bar...** from the Insert menu.
2. Jump to the Navigation Type tab, and select the "Custom" option. The Customize tab is automatically displayed.
3. Rearrange the order of the navigation bar items by drag and drop (or use the **Move Up**, **Move Down**, **Make Child** or **Make Parent** buttons.
4. Click the **Add Element** button to add a new element to the end of your navigation bar list. The element is assigned a link destination, a target frame or window and a title in the displayed dialog. Click **OK**.
5. Click **OK** again.

Any selected element in the customize window can be edited or deleted.

Adding Java applets

Java is a cross-platform, object-oriented programming language used to create mini-applications called **applets** that can be attached to Web pages and that run when the page is viewed in a Web browser. WebPlus lets you add Java applets to your Web sites. You don't have to write your own! Plenty of applets are available online—for example animation, interface components, live information updating, two-way interaction, graphics rendering, live updating, streaming audio and video, games, and many more.

Downloaded applets typically consist of a main ".class" file and one or more associated files (such as other .class files, picture files, media files, etc.).

Again, you don't need to understand the underlying code, but it's essential to make sense of any "Read Me" documentation that comes with the applet. When using WebPlus to embed an applet, you must list its component files as well as any necessary parameters (as described in the applet's documentation) that specify exactly how the applet should run.

When adding a Java applet in WebPlus, you have the option of **embedding** its files in your project, as opposed to keeping them separate. Although embedding any file adds to the size of the project, it is the default option because you'll no longer have to worry about juggling separate files or the chance of accidentally deleting one of them. When you publish your site, WebPlus takes care of exporting and copying both embedded and non-embedded files.

Bear in mind that Java applets won't execute instantly in a visitor's browser. As with image or media files, it will take time to download the applet files to the user's computer before anything "happens" on screen. Take the combined applet file sizes into account when figuring the time it will take the Web page to display.

WebPlus inserts a marker into your site at the place where the applet will appear on your Web page. You can't actually see the applet running until you preview the exported site. The marker's dimensions probably won't correspond exactly to those of the applet when it's running, so plan your page layout accordingly. Also, bear in mind that a Java applet's user interface may look slightly different on each browser that displays it, even on the same operating system. The more preview tests you can run, for example using both Netscape Navigator and Microsoft Internet Explorer, the better.

To add a Java applet to a page:

1. Click the **Insert Java Applet** button on the Web Objects toolbar's Media flyout.
2. In the dialog, click **Browse...** to locate and select a specific Applet Class File or archive file (.JAR or .ZIP). If the latter is specified, you have to select which .class file should be run from within the archive file.
3. Click the upper **Add..** button to locate any other files required by the applet. You can hold down the **Ctrl** or **Shift** key to select multiple files in the dialog. To delete a file once you've added it to your list, click the file name and then click the **Delete** button.
4. If you do not wish to embed the files in your project, uncheck the "Embed" option.

5. Click the lower **Add...** button to enter any required parameters (see documentation supplied with the Java applet). Add parameters one at a time, typing the Name and Value (excluding quotation marks) in the fields provided.

   To delete a parameter from the list (for example if you typed it wrong), click the **Up** or **Down** buttons to select the parameter, then click the **Delete** button below the list.

6. Click **OK** to close the dialog, then click (or click and drag) with the cursor to place the Java marker on your page.

When you publish your site, WebPlus will export and copy both embedded and non-embedded files into a common folder along with the HTML pages and graphics. Keep this in mind when entering file paths. If the applet's documentation insists on certain components being placed into separate subdirectories, you'll need to place them there "by hand" using an FTP utility.

WebPlus Advanced

10

Creating HTML pages

HTML code is the underlying tagged code which your web site visitor's Internet browser reads, interprets and formats your page according to the tags used. The code and tags used are the instructions to which a page will be formatted, and as such it is vital that the code is correctly structured and conforms to HTML convention.

WebPlus supports the development of web pages in pure W3C-compliant HTML. You can add pages within the Site tab's Site Structure window—a distinct HTML page icon is shown.

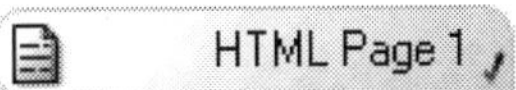

HTML pages in the Site tab can be controlled in a similar way to standard pages, i.e. you can drag/drop, rename, preview, insert offline links to, estimate download time for any page. However, HTML pages do not have master pages associated with them, In addition, a double-click of the HTML page icon will launch the HTML page's Source window for HTML editing (rather than the WYSIWYG display of a standard page). In the Source window you'll see some basic HTML tags which, if you're an experienced HTML developer, will be very familiar to you!

```
<html>
<head>
<title></title>
</head>
<body>

</body>
</html>
```

There is no WYSIWYG view when you work with HTML source code directly.

From this point, a text-based edit of the "template" HTML structure is required. Body text can be pasted between the <body> and </body> tags, with each paragraph beginning and ending in <p> and </p>, respectively. It's worth noting that editing HTML code requires prior understanding of HTML language and its convention. Poor editing may result in corruption of your code on the page or site level.

If you're new to HTML and need to start with the basics, it's best to search for "HTML tutorials" in your favourite Internet search engine before tackling HTML editing in earnest.

To create an HTML page:

- Right-click a page in your Site tab and select **Insert HTML page...**.
  OR

  Click the **Site Structure** button just above the Site Structure tree (or on the HintLine), or choose **Site Structure...** from the File menu. In the dialog, select a page and click the **Html page...** button (optionally as a child of the selected page).

A new page is added after the right-clicked page to the Site tab.

To edit an HTML page's source:

- Double-click the HTML page icon in the Site tab's Site Structure and edit the displayed code.

To change HTML page properties:

- Right-click on the HTML page icon in the Site tab, and pick Page Properties.
- From the dialog, uncheck **Include in Navigation** so the page does not appear in navigation bars.
- Click the **Change...** button to rename the HTML page's file name.

Attaching HTML code

In WebPlus, you can create pages in pure HTML (see **Creating HTML pages** on p. 165). However, WebPlus also lets you attach code to your WebPlus objects and pages, primarily to expand the capabilities of the objects (or the page), making them more intelligent and interactive. This can be done in three ways—you can attach code to the source of:

- a self-inserted HTML fragment
- a specific object placed on the page
- an entire page

It's not possible to edit the HTML code itself (there's no real benefit in doing so), but specific areas of the displayed code are editable for additional code to be added, i.e. clearly identifiable placeholders (shown in green text colour) will appear in your source tab's window.

```
__AddCode="here"
```

```
<!--Header code for
```

```
<!--Preamble-->
```

```
<!--MainDivStart-->
```

```
<!--MainDivEnd-->
```

```
<!--Postamble-->
```

```
<!--Body-->
```

```
<!--Page Body Start-->
```

These are just a few of the **editable** placeholders present in the source of an HTML fragment, object or page (in fact differently named placeholders exist depending on the type of element). For example, the last placeholder shown in the list above is unique to a page's source and won't appear for an object or HTML fragment.

Any code can be inserted by cut and paste into any of the placeholder positions but typically you can include tokens, HTML code or specific scripts, e.g. JavaScript. This could be used to affect rollover behaviour on an object not otherwise possible without scripting support, e.g. an image "on-click" handler.

Adding HTML

WebPlus also allows you to add extra **HTML code** to a page. Using this approach, you can include fragments either copied from another Web page, or perhaps written by yourself.

You can also import formatted HTML text from a browser or email program via the Clipboard (for example with a browser's **Select All** and **Copy** commands), using WebPlus's **File>Paste Special...** command. Using the **Import Web Pages** option, you can import one or more HTML pages into your new or existing WebPlus site, with control over which additional elements are imported.

When you import HTML code, WebPlus inserts a marker into your site at the site where the code will be placed. Since you won't be able to see the effect of the HTML until you **preview** the site, be careful to place the marker correctly. You'll definitely want to check your Web page in a browser! If there's a problem, double-check the code you entered and its position on the WebPlus page. If you have some grasp of HTML, examine the page source in a text editor such as Notepad or use your browser's "View Source" mode.

To add an HTML code fragment to a page:

1. Click the **Insert HTML Code** button on the Web Objects toolbar.
2. Click on the page or pasteboard to create a new HTML Code Fragment window at a default size or drag to adjust the window's dimensions.
3. In the dialog, use the **Paste to Head** or **Paste to Body** button to insert the clipboard text into the header of the file or into its body.
OR
Use the scrollable code window. Enter one or more HTML code fragments into the appropriate field.
4. If the code calls for external files, use the **Add** button to locate them. Click the **Embed** button if you want to keep the file(s) separate from your project file.
5. Click **OK** to close the dialog, then click (or click and drag) with the cursor to place the HTML marker on your page.

Adding JavaScript

To source a vast array of JavaScript code, try searching for "javascript snippets" in your favourite search engine. You should find many thousands of sites hosting freely available code snippets. Most of these sites will clearly indicate what the JavaScript will do for you—they'll also normally let you select the JavaScript code and copy it for pasting into an HTML fragment's, object's or page's Source window, HTML table cell or directly onto the page.

Here are some typical uses when applying code to your web pages.

- Disable right-mouse click on page objects
- Add a Print current page button
- Add a date and time to your page
- Change an object's colour when selected

Let's look at how to add some of JavaScript (sourced or written by yourself if you've experience of JavaScript programming).

To illustrate, compare the two pieces of example code below. A very simple JavaScript code snippet is added to the Source window which will display the current date on your web page. The first section of code uses the last placeholder in the above list (*<!--Page Body Start-->*), the second how the code looks after a script has replaced the placeholder.

Code showing placeholder

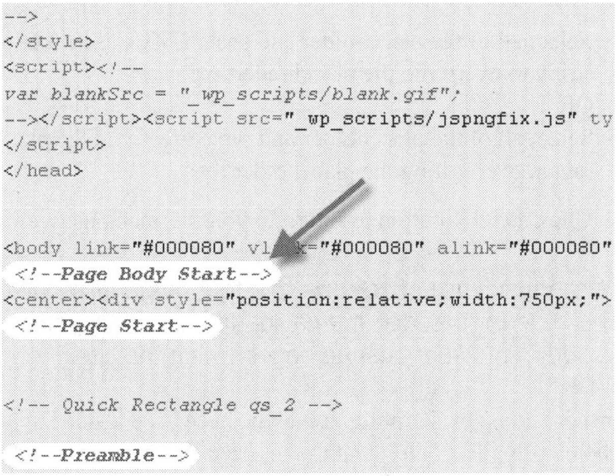

```
-->
</style>
<script><!--
var blankSrc = "_wp_scripts/blank.gif";
--></script><script src="_wp_scripts/jspngfix.js" ty
</script>
</head>


<body link="#000080" vlink="#000080" alink="#000080"
<!--Page Body Start-->
<center><div style="position:relative;width:750px;">
<!--Page Start-->


<!-- Quick Rectangle qs_2 -->

<!--Preamble-->
```

Code after added JavaScript

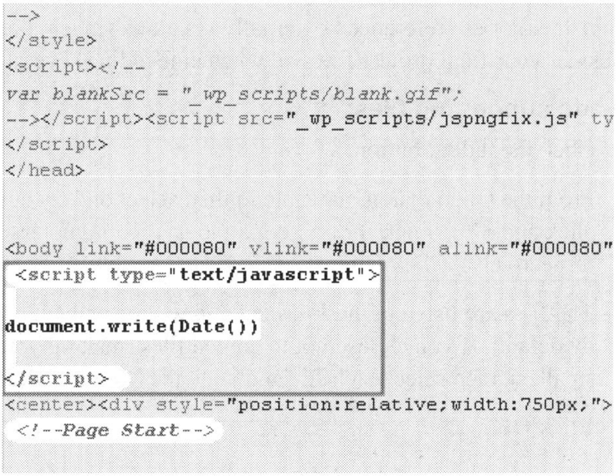

```
-->
</style>
<script><!--
var blankSrc = "_wp_scripts/blank.gif";
--></script><script src="_wp_scripts/jspngfix.js" ty
</script>
</head>


<body link="#000080" vlink="#000080" alink="#000080"
<script type="text/javascript">

document.write(Date())

</script>
<center><div style="position:relative;width:750px;">
<!--Page Start-->
```

This simple example illustrates where simple code is placed in a source window.

To attach code to an HTML fragment or object:

1. Select an existing HTML fragment or object.
2. From the Format menu, select **Attach HTML...**.
   OR
   Right-click on the object and choose the same option.
3. In the dialog, scroll the source window to locate editable placeholders. Which placeholder you choose depends on what you want to achieve.
4. Select all of the placeholder and paste HTML, script or any other text string to overwrite the placeholder text.
   OR
   Select all of the placeholder and type directly in the placeholder's location (again overwriting the placeholder text).
5. Click the **OK** button to return to your normal page view.

> You can make use of **tokens** to add a range of variables to your HTML. Use for breadcrumb navigation that will update dynamically if you add, remove or change pages within the site.

For more complex scripting, it may be necessary to add supporting files (graphics, text files, etc.) that the inserted script may use—these can be either embedded or linked. This means the files are either kept with the WPP project (embedded) or are referenced externally via a link (much like a hyperlink). Consider your final project file size when embedding several images.

To add supporting files:

1. Click the **Add...** button.
2. From the Open dialog, navigate to then select one or more files (use **Ctrl**-click and **Shift**-click for non-contiguous or contiguous selection, respectively). Click **Open**.
3. The files are listed in the **Files** list and will be embedded in your project by default. If you choose not to embed files (making your project smaller), then select each file and click the **Make Linked** button.
4. Click **OK**.

At any point, you can **Add**, **Delete**, and change **Export Options** for any file.

To attach code to a page:

1. Right-click on the page and choose **Attach HTML...**.
   OR
   Choose the **Attach HTML** button on the Standard toolbar.
2. In the dialog, scroll the window to locate editable placeholders. Which placeholder you choose depends on what you want to achieve.
3. Select all of the placeholder and paste HTML, script or any other text string to overwrite the placeholder text.
   OR
   Select all of the placeholder and type directly in the placeholder's location (again overwriting the placeholder text).
4. To switch back to your normal page view, click the project tab at the top of the source window.

Using IDs

All objects in WebPlus are given unique alphanumeric IDs for referencing by scripting languages. By default, ID generation is automatic for each object, text column, table row and table cell. For example, a newly drawn QuickShape will automatically be assigned an ID of "qs_1", a second QuickShape will be "qs_2", pictures could be "pic_1", "pic_2", etc.

It may be perfectly acceptable to utilize these automatic IDs in your scripts but if you need to assign your own IDs, it's possible to turn off the site-wide automatic generation of IDs in the **Options** tab of the Site Properties dialog (select **Site Properties...** from the File menu). Uncheck the option specific for object, text column, table row and/or table cell and press **OK**. Your own replacement IDs can instead be added in the available placeholder, i.e.

```
AddCode="here"
```

If the object is copied on the same page or to another web site, the ID number will be replaced by a new ID number.

Any object ID can be edited once the object is on the web page. A different name can be used or, if you don't want to show an object's ID (but want to keep site-wide ID generation), you can prevent the ID from being shown in source code.

To edit an object ID:

1. Right-click an object and select **ID**.
   OR
   Select the object and choose **HTML ID...** from the Format menu.
2. In the dialog, modify the HTML ID value.
3. (Optional) Choose whether to **Write ID for this object**. Selecting "Use Site default" means that the setting in the **Options** tab of the Site Properties dialog is honoured—"Yes" or "No" means that the object's ID is always shown or never shown irrespective of the site default setting.

Tokens

WebPlus provides a range of grouped HTML annotation tokens which can be attached to HTML fragments, objects or pages. They get replaced by appropriate "real" values when you export to a file or preview your page.

Adding tokens is a simple case of inserting a token string, by copy and paste or typing directly, into one of the placeholder positions in any HTML source.

A full list of such tokens is provided in the WebPlus Help (search for tokens in the Index).

Forms

Web-based forms allow information to be collected from visitors to your web site in an efficient and modern manner. In much the same way as traditional paper forms are used to collect information, Web-based forms offer the same form completion concepts, but take advantage of the Internet as a powerful information conduit.

Some common form types are:

- Application forms
- Contact Information forms
- Request forms
- Subscription forms
- Feedback forms
- Guest books

Form data can be collected in a variety of ways—by email, to a text file, database, or via **Serif Web Resources**, a web service for transferring form data to customer email addresses.

Form Structure

The building blocks of a form comprise a mixture of text, graphics and **form controls**. Form controls are intelligent as they collect web visitor data and can be added, moved and modified in a similar way to familiar objects in WebPlus such as graphics and table elements. A field can be a Button, Box, Text Area, Combo box, Check box, Radio Button, or File browser. A typical form is made up of a combination of these fields, i.e.

From the web visitor's perspective, information is typed into text boxes or selected from check boxes, radio buttons, or drop-down boxes. The information entered can be numeric, textual, or a mixture of both, depending on the type of field.

Each field has its own set of properties relating to its appearance, its value(s), validation, or the action expected of the field.

In WebPlus, the form should be integrated into your site design as you develop your site. The form's functionality only then becomes active when your web site is published (of course you can still preview your forms from within WebPlus, see **Previewing your Web site** on p. 209). When a web visitor enters data into, or selects a form option, the data will be sent back to a chosen destination when the form is submitted.

Where is data sent?

After submission, form data can be sent to one of the following:

- an email address
- a script file (stored locally or remotely); this could write text to a text file or into a server database
- **Serif Web Resources**; for transit of form data to your email (via Serif).

As is standard in Web form management, it is possible to set the encoding type, target window/frames, submission methods (POST or GET) can be used.

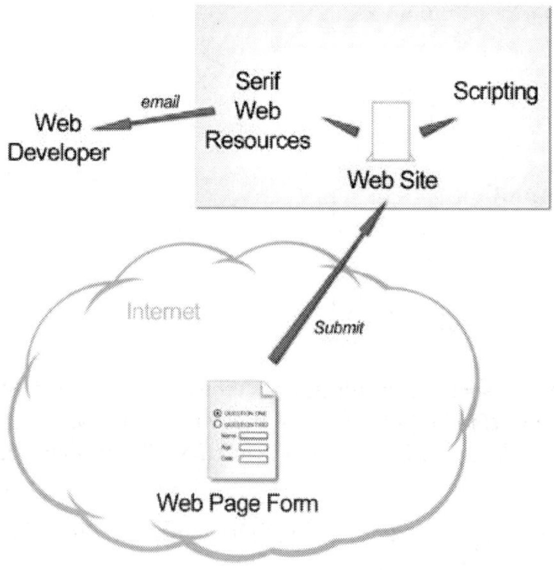

Using Standard Forms

If you're still confused by forms as a concept you don't need to panic! WebPlus comes complete with a range of ready-to-go standard forms. Alternatively, standard web form objects, acting as building blocks for your form, can be adopted to modify existing forms or create your own forms. For ready-to-go forms there's no need to add form controls, submission buttons, form control validation or perform time-consuming form design work—it's already done for you!

Using JavaScript

JavaScript can be used to allow interactivity in your Web forms. It drives formatting, validation, calculations, and actions—all key functions in Web-based form development.

Creating forms

Several methods exist for creating forms dependent on whether you wish to be helped with a WebForm Wizard, use standard forms (i.e., pre-defined ready-to-go forms supplied with WebPlus), or create a form from scratch. Whichever method is chosen will depend on the level of customization you want to go to—as a rule of thumb, it's always best to familiarize yourself with WebPlus's standard forms that could be used first. This may save you time, and allow you to create your form more easily.

To create a form (via WebForm Wizard):

1. Click the **Insert Form Wizard** on the Web Objects toolbar's Forms flyout.
2. In the dialog, click the **Create a new form with the wizard** icon and then **Next>**.
3. In the next screen, you need to add **form controls** that will make up your form. In the Add box, click on your chosen form control. See **Form controls** on p. 178 for a detailed description of each control.

Want to speed up design? Use the **Pre-defined** button to adopt a wide range of ready-to-go form components.

4. In the form control's **Add New Control** dialog use the internal name for the control (to uniquely identify it), or edit it and enter a label to accompany the control (this is shown on-screen). The **Add New Control** dialog also lets you edit the control and its label—use the **Edit Control...** or **Edit Label...** button, respectively. Editing a control allows validation, control of form length, and other control attributes to be set. See **Editing form controls** on p. 178 for more information. If you've edited a value, click **OK**.

5. Repeat the above two steps as necessary for each chosen form control. They will be listed (in order of creation) in the upper window. Before continuing, you have to add a Submit form control to your form. This is vital to pass data to its destination. Click the **Submit Button** to automatically add the button to your form. It is normal practice to accompany this with a **Reset Button**, used to clear out form fields of data not yet submitted.
   Click **Next>**.

6. From the next screen, choose a destination for your form data by clicking a destination button for email, script file (local or remote) and **Serif Web Resources** and a name to define the whole form. (See **Submission of forms** on p. 182). Select **Finish** to complete the wizard.

7. To insert the form at a default size, position the form place cursor where you want the form to appear on the page, then simply click the mouse.

If you prefer a different approach, you can add a Standard form. Standard forms are pre-defined forms for Contact information, User comments, CV submission, Opinion, and Address forms to name a few. You can also build up standard forms from a gallery of single or multiple pre-defined form objects (see To create a form from scratch below).

To create a standard form:

1. Click the **Insert Form Wizard** on the Web Objects toolbar's Forms flyout.

2. In the dialog, click the **Use and adapt a standard form** icon and then **Next>**.

3. From the list of forms, select a form type while using the Preview pane.

4. Click **Next>**.

5. In the next screen, choose to add, modify or delete.

- To add, click a button in the **Add** box.
- To modify a standard object, select an existing control in the window and choose **Edit Control...**. See **Editing form controls** on p. 181 for more information.
- To delete a standard object, select an existing control in the window and choose **Delete**.
- To rearrange the control order, use the **Move Up** and **Move Down** buttons.

6. From the next screen, choose a destination for your form data by clicking a destination button. Select **Finish** to complete the wizard.
7. To insert the form at a default size, position the form place cursor and click the mouse.

If you're looking for design freedom, WebPlus provides a blank form and form objects from which you can design your form from scratch. You can add form controls or standard form objects, or both.

To create a form from scratch:

1. Click the **Insert Blank Form** button on the Web Objects toolbar's Forms flyout. You'll see the mouse pointer change to the **Form Paste** cursor. What you do next determines the initial size and placement of the form.
2. To insert the form at a default size, simply click the mouse. The created form is composed of a grey form area and a Submit button.
   OR
   To set the size of the inserted form, drag out a region and release the mouse button.

Once the blank form is established, form controls or standard web form objects can be added to the form area, i.e.

- From the Web Objects toolbar's Forms flyout, drag any one of the **form controls**, e.g. an Edit Box, directly onto the grey form area, positioning the control using rulers, the grid or guides.
  OR

1. Click the **Insert Standard Form Object** button on the Web Objects toolbar's Forms flyout.
2. From the dialog, choose a category, and select a form object from the category list, e.g. a countries drop-down menu. Click **OK**.
3. To insert the object, position the form place cursor over the form area, then click the mouse.
   OR

- Right-click on a standard form and choose **Form Wizard...**.

Standard form objects, when selected, can be edited by clicking the **Edit Standard Form Object** button on the Web Objects toolbar's Forms flyout.

As we're looking at forms and in particular form objects in more detail, let's take a more in-depth look at form controls.

Form controls

Each form control is an "intelligent" object which differs from other WebPlus objects. They can be moved as for other objects but cannot have colours or transparency applied, borders adjusted, or resized. They are intelligent because they can store user input and pass it on to a central location during form submission.

A range of form controls are available from within the **WebForm Wizard** or directly from the Web Objects toolbar (or via the **Form** option on the Insert menu). You assign an internal unique name to each field and then set a variety of **properties**—each form control has its own set which can be modified.

Web Objects Toolbar Icon	Form Control Name	When to use?
	Form Button	Use when specifying an action that can be triggered by a button click. A whole range of buttons of varying design and function can be created. Some uses include: • *Advanced* - Displays menu options that are only applicable for advanced uses. • *Show All* - Displays all menu options. • *Next page* - Jumps to the next page. • *Open* - Opens a file or Web link. • *Import* - Imports form data. Note that *Submit* and *Reset* buttons are available in the WebForm wizard. They perform form submission and clear all form data, respectively.
	Edit Box	Use for entering single-line text, numbers, or a mixture of both. Someone's surname or insurance number would be a good example.
	Text Area	Use for adding multi-line text, numbers or a mixture of both. Generally used for entering input, either textual or numerical, e.g. an enquiry, recipe, or list of figures.
	Combo Box	For selection from a list of items in a drop-down menu where only one item can be selected by default, e.g. a gender combo.  Combo boxes also allow for a scrollable list of items; with optional support for multiple selection. For example, to select Afghanistan, Algeria, and Andorra, use Ctrl-click on each item:

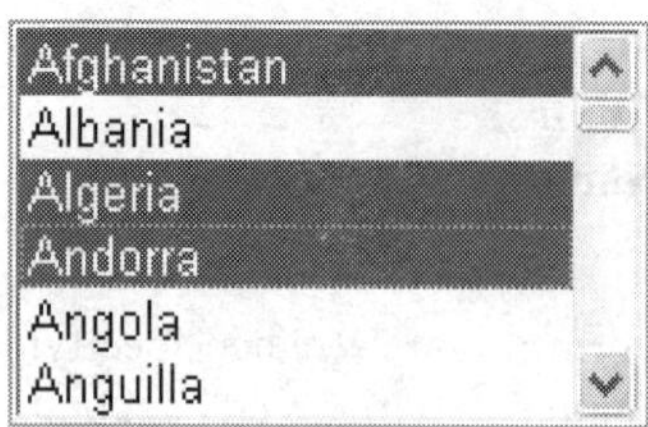

You can use Shift-click to group select a range of items.

For multiple selection, drag the top or bottom of the Combo box to allow several items to bc displayed by default.

	Check Box	Ideal when you want to multiply select a series of items displayed side by side. A good alternative to a Combo Box if space allows. The web visitor clicks once to select or deselect the box, e.g. *Would you like to be notified of any upcoming events in the near future?*
	Radio Button	Good for selection of a single mutually exclusive item from a grouped subset of choices. For example, a set of radio buttons can be used to obtain gender information from the web visitor. Male Female
	File Browser	Use the File browser to have your web visitors upload any file from their computers. The visitor simply navigates via a **Browse...** button and select the file of their choice. Some examples include uploading pictures, CVs, drawings and instructions.

Hidden objects can be added as a form control if you use the WebForm Wizard. Although the web visitor does not see the field it is typically used by the web developer to ensure the data collected has an identifiable string stored with the user's data. An example could be a publish date relating to the web page—useful for identifying incorrectly working pages.

In addition, hidden fields can be added by right-clicking on the entire form and selecting **Edit Form Properties...**. The dialog's **Hidden Fields** tab allows for input of any number of hidden fields.

Editing form controls

Each form control type (buttons, text field, etc.) has different characteristics and therefore different values for editing. Values can be changed as you create the form or at a later time after the control has been added to the form. Typically you may want to:

- change the internally stored control **Name** and its **Initial Value** (what gets displayed on-screen by default).
- treat the control's value as script (check to preserve initial value's script content instead of converting it to HTML).
- set a **Maximum length** for the field (use as a type of validation).
- set the field to **Disabled**. Check to make the control inactive unless activated by script.
- set an **Access** key. Jump to the form control with a keyboard shortcut (use with Alt key and keyboard letter).
- make a control **Read only** (check to make control non-editable unless changed by script). Could be conditional on other fields being completed.
- create a control suitable for a **Password** (web visitor input is masked).

The WebForm Wizard's **Edit Control...** button lets you modify the control during form creation. Alternatively, the control can be edited later by right-clicking on the form control on the web page and choosing the Edit option, e.g. Edit Text Box.

Combo Box editing

Editing a combo box is a little more complicated than other fields. The combo Box needs to be populated with multiple entries to create selection choices within the box. In the From Combo Box dialog, use **Add Options...** to sequentially build up your menu entries—this involves adding name and value pairs one-by-one (use the Add Another button to speed up the process).

Any Combo Box will support **Groups**. This means you can categorize entries into common groupings for easier navigation. While the group itself is not selectable you can make more sense of a long list of entries by creating the group name (click **Add Group...**) and moving entries under the group with the **Make Child** button (position entry under the chosen group). For example, a country Combo Box could be categorized by continent.

Radio Box editing

Radio box from controls operate slightly differently to other form controls. To operate correctly, Radio buttons which are intended to be grouped, must both be configured to be a part of the same configurable **Group Name**. Simply create a group name for the first radio button and adopt that name for any other radio buttons intended for that group.

Submission of forms

All forms have one thing in common—they must be submitted to allow data to be collected. To do this you can either create a **Submit Button** unaided or more usually use the ready-made button in the WebForm Wizard. The button needs to be present on the form and is typically used with a Reset button to clear all form controls of data.

No action

Form data is not submitted. This option is useful if you want to temporarily disable data collection or if you haven't set up scripting or Serif Web Resources. At a later time to can edit the form (right-click then choose **Edit Form Properties**) and select a valid submission method.

Serif Web Resources

Not everyone will have access to or even want to operate their own Web server so, as an alternative, you can use **Serif Web Resources**. This is a free Web to email gateway service which will transit your valued form data via Serif and send it to your personal email address—the service does require that you firstly have a Serif Web resources login (for security reasons), which will allow you to create, edit and delete your own email destinations, these are called Form Email Targets.

To set up Serif Web Resources:

1. With the **Serif Web Resources** icon enabled, add a Form name.
2. Click the **Select** button and login to Serif Web Resources.
3. From the dialog, enter your destination email in the **New Target** box and click **Add New Target**. The email entry is created and added to the available email address list—with the email address selected, click **OK**. You'll notice that the entry is classed as "*Not Confirmed*". Before the service commences, you'll get a email confirmation message sent to your email address. By clicking the link, the service will be activated and the entry will change to "*Confirmed*".
4. Choose a submission method, encoding type, and target window/frame.

You can remove an entry by selecting it and clicking **Remove Target**.

You may be wondering what typical form data might look like once sent through Serif Web Resources. Here's an example of data collected from a simple form.

Time Submitted: Thu, 01 Jun 2006 17:45:10 BST
Referrer:
From IP: 80.6.91.225
firstname = Doug
lastname = Walker
gender = Male
info = Social Events

No personal data will be stored on Serif Web servers. All form data is redirected in real time.

Script file

This option is for experienced web developers with scripting expertise. Typically a script file is written and stored along with WebPlus's other web pages and is uploaded during the **Publish to the World Wide Web** operation.

If uploading to an ISP, it's essential to check with your ISP in advance if scripting is allowed on your web space. If not, you will have to adopt another solution, perhaps choosing another ISP that allow scripting or choose a script file hosted on your ISP (most provide a simple script; you would use the **Remote script** option below for this). If in doubt, contact your ISP if you're not sure.

To set up a local script file:

1. With the **Script file** icon enabled, add a Form name.
2. Navigate to your local script file, typically a .CGI, .PL, .DLL, or .EXE file with the **Browse** button.
3. Check **Embed** to include the script within the WebPlus project. If unchecked, the script file will be unconnected to the project (any updates to the script will be invisible to the project).
4. Optionally, the **Export Options...** button lets you define a web file name and folder for the script.
5. Choose a submission method, encoding type, and target window/frame.

Remote script

Use if your ISP will not allow you to run your own scripts on your ISP web space. Instead, your ISP may supply a basic script file that can be linked to from your web page. Typically, the script will send the form data back to your email address (already setup with your ISP).

To set up a remote script file:

1. With the **Remote script** icon enabled, add a Form name.
2. Enter a URL pointing directly to a script file, typically a .CGI, .PL, .DLL, or .EXE file.
3. Choose a submission method, encoding type, and target window/frame.

email address

Use this option to bypass the usual POST/GET submission methods. When the Submit button is pressed the web visitor's default email program is launched. The form data (passed in a single string) is added to the email body and is ready to be sent to the configured email destination. Especially useful if there is no local or remote scripting in place.

 This is an unsecure submission method—any private or confidential information will be not be encrypted.

To set up email directly:

1. With the **email address** icon enabled, add a Form name.
2. Enter the destination email address in the drop-down menu.

As the data is sent in a string you may have to disassemble the string into more manageable and useable text. Applying a script, e.g., a Microsoft Word macro, would be one solution.

 You cannot use the File browser feature when using this submission method. Instead add the file as an attachment directly within your email program.

You can set a default subject line by entering a subject line string after your normal email address, e.g.

fred.walker@hotmail.com?subject=New%20Contact%Details

Where %20 is used to include a space character.

This is a great way of identifying form-generated emails entering your inbox—the subject line will always be "New Contact Details." Additionally, try an email filter on "New Contact Details" to automatically sort "form" emails from usual emails.

To set up the submission method (POST or GET), encoding type or target window/frames see WebPlus help.

Arranging tab order

Web visitors have two options for navigating their web forms—by clicking in each field in turn (using the mouse) or using the Tab key to jump from field to field. The latter method is more efficient as web forms are generally designed to be completed in a sequential manner.

This tab sequence is controlled by the order in which the form designer adds the form fields to the page during the design process. Clearly, the form design may change during development so the tab order is prone to getting out of sequence. Fortunately, the tab order be changed at any time.

To change tab order:

1. Click the **Tab Order** button on the Web Objects toolbar's Forms flyout. This reveals numbered tab markers on all your form controls.
2. Sequentially, click on the form fields in the order in which you want them to be assigned tab numbers. This automatically assigns a new tab number to the marker—your first click will be to assign 1 in First Name field, the second click 2 in the Last Name field, etc.

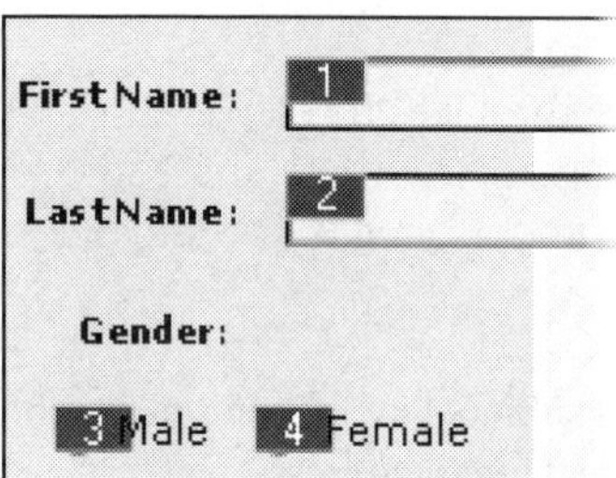

3. Click the **Tab Order** button again to switch off the tab markers.

If you're not happy with the order you've assigned, click the Tab Order button and start again.

You can also right-click a form and choose **Change Tab Order** from the menu. Tab markers are shown and can be changed as before. Click the form to switch off makers.

 Remember to include any Submit and Reset buttons in the Tab Order.

Validating data entry

During or after designing your form it is possible to apply some data entry rules, i.e. validation, on your form controls. The main objective is to ensure that the form is filled out correctly and ensures that data is useable. This is done by checking that user's data entered into each field is of the correct format, structure and sequence. If not, the user is informed of this via a pop-up message, which is configurable.

If data entry is not correct the form cannot be submitted until validation is successful.

To set form control validation:

1. Right-click on the form control and choose the Edit option (e.g., Edit Form Text Box). For each form control this is different.
2. Jump to the Validation tab, and check appropriate validation for the form control, i.e.
   - For Edit Boxes, check if the box must be filled, a number only, or email address only. You can also restrict the number range that the web visitor can input by setting a Minimum value and Maximum value.
   - For Text Area, check if the area must be filled.
   - For Combo Boxes, check if a selection must be made.
   - For Check boxes, check if a check box must be checked.
   - For the File browser, check if a file must be uploaded.
3. Each check box is accompanied by a message box. Enter a supporting message to help your web visitor complete the form control successfully.

Custom Validation with JavaScript

For Edit Boxes, more advanced validation on forms can be performed within WebPlus. It's possible to write your own JavaScript code and apply it in the Custom validation script window (see **Attaching HTML code** on p. 166). When the form control is completed by the web visitor, the custom script is run and validation is carried out.

Some examples of custom validation include:

- the blocking of swear words.
- Specifying account numbers with a set structure (e.g., EM 158 3466 7546//2).

The development of JavaScript code is outside the scope of this User Guide. To get started with writing JavaScript, try one of the many tutorials available on the Internet (search your favourite search engine for "beginning javascript").

Using Smart Objects

It's quite common for web developers to "inherit" content from existing web sites to save time and effort, while bearing in mind any legal implications in doing so. This is fine for simple graphic or text copying, but this process is not possible for more complex, interactive objects such as counters, shout boxes, blogs, etc, which collect information with the object. The power of, for example, a hit counter lies in its ability to keep a count of the number of users that have visited a page at all times. The count needs to be stored somewhere and herein lies the problem. Storing object data (counts, chat text, blog text, is not always encouraged or even supported on ISP web space—due to potential security breaches and disk usage demands. So where can the data be stored?

To resolve the problem for Serif WebPlus users, WebPlus can place such objects, called **Smart Objects**, on the page and also store associated object data on Serif's own secure server space. These objects are available from **Serif Web Resources** a secure online service for obtaining objects and storing data at the same time.

An advantage of using Serif's Smart Objects is that they are optimized and fully tested for use in your current WebPlus project. In addition, the objects are hosted online so new updates may be added over time.

Let's look at each Smart Object you'll find in Web Resources and what you can do with them.

Name	Use
Active Viewers	Use to show how many people are currently viewing the web page.
Blog	A blog (short for weblog) acts as a personal journal on your web page and is frequently updated (often daily) with articles. Articles are typically commented on by visitors to the web page.
Hit Counter	A straightforward count of the number of hits on the current page. Different styles can be adopted.
Mailing List	Have users sign up to newsletters, party confirmations, information request, and many more, by collection of web visitor's emails as required.
Poll	Set up a online poll to canvass web visitor's opinions.
Shout Box	Acts as a interactive chat window similar to Windows Messenger. Let your web visitors chat amongst themselves.

For security reasons, the objects are only available via a Serif **Web Resources** login accessible from within WebPlus. If you don't have a valid username and password you must create a Web Resources account first.

- If your email address is already known to Serif (maybe you've just registered or have registered previously) you'll be asked for a limited number of questions to completed account registration.
- If you're new to Serif and unregistered you'll have to complete full security as required. Full instructions are provided on login screens.

By the way, you may have come across Serif Web Resources if you've been using WebPlus 10's **forms functionality** (see p. 172). The form submission process allows form data to be emailed via Serif Web Resources to a specified mail address. The same login can be used but a different area of Web Resources is displayed if either forms or Smart Objects are to be used.

To create a Serif Web Resources account:

1. Click the **Smart Object Tool** button on the Web Objects toolbar.
2. In the login dialog, click the **Create Account** link under the login boxes.
3. In the next dialog, enter your current email address and a password twice.
4. Click the **Signup** button.
5. An additional dialog, will ask for personal details, plus a few check boxes if you would like to receive the Serif Community newsletter, Serif offers, and/or other third-party offers.
6. A confirmation email will be sent to your email address. Click the link in the email and you're ready to access Web Resources.

To clear Account details:

- Go to **Tools>Options** and click **Clear Account Details** shown from the General option. This will clear the stored login details for Serif Web Resources so that automatic login will no longer work. Details will need to be entered next time so be sure you've remembered your password.

To access Web Resources:

1. Click the **Smart Object Tool** button on the Web Objects toolbar.
2. At the login prompt enter your username and your password. Select **Remember account details** to access Web Resources directly in future (bypassing the login screen).
3. Click the **Login** button. The Smart Objects dialog is displayed.

Creating Smart Objects

Think of a Smart Object as being a general term for elements that you'll use on your page—as discussed previously. The actual creation of such an object is quite painless. Smart Objects are not added directly to the page from Serif Web Resources, but are first added to your own object library (the library lets you manage and edit each object)—objects can then be added to the web page immediately or at a later date.

To add an object to the library:

1. Select the **New...** button at the bottom of the My Smart Objects Library pane.
2. In the **Create Smart Object** dialog, use the scroll bar to navigate the list of Smart Objects, hover over an object of interest and click.
3. Select **OK**.
4. Depending on the type of object selected, a different Create dialog will be displayed. For example, creating a Blog will show a **Create New Blog** dialog. This reflects the difference in each object's characteristics.
5. Change the **Name** of the object and optionally a **Filter Offsite** string (this prevents the URL from being copied). Optionally, change the object specific settings, e.g. for some objects you can also set the titling, colours (for body, text and border), and border thickness if appropriate.
6. Click **OK**.

The named object will be shown in a list in the My Smart Objects left-hand pane, i.e.

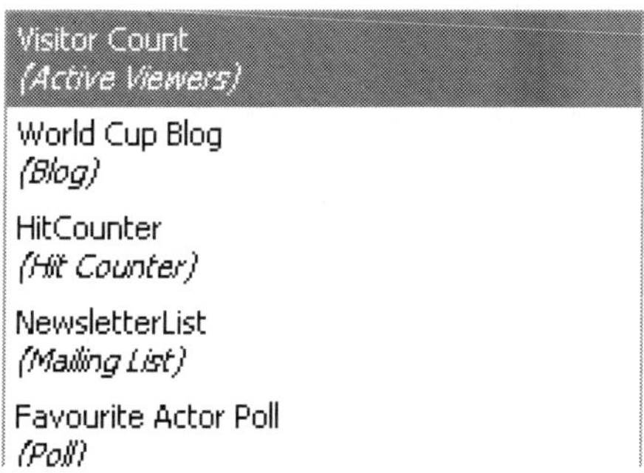

For example, the currently selected Visitor Count object has just been added to an existing list of Smart Objects.

To add a Smart Object to your web page:

1. From the dialog, select the chosen object from the left-hand pane and click the **Insert** button.
2. To insert the object at a default size, position the cursor where you want the object to appear on the page, then simply click the mouse.

The object added to your page may not look as you expect—you'll need to **preview** Smart Objects to see them properly.

Editing Smart Objects

Once an object is created it can be edited either in the My Smart Object Library or directly on the page. Typically, you might want to alter the appearance of the object from its the originally settings, maybe change a Poll question, or reset a Hit Counter back to zero.

Editing an object only affects the object itself and does not alter any collected data.

The dialog options for editing and creating a Smart Object are the same, except that the object's Name is read only (shown as greyed out) in the object edit dialogs.

To edit a Smart Object in your library:

1. Click the **Smart Object Tool** button on the Web Objects toolbar and login.
2. Select a Smart Object for edit from the My Smart Objects Library pane.
3. In the adjacent window, select the Edit... button under the object preview.

The selected object's edit dialog is displayed.

To edit a Smart Object on your page:

- Double-click the object to reveal the object's Edit dialog.
  OR
- Right-click the object and select **Edit Smart Object...**.

If you edit an object on the web page the change is also reflected in the Objects library and vice versa.

Managing Smart Objects

While editing Smart Objects affects only the object as a "container", managing Smart Objects can be used to manage the object's data. Some Smart Objects such as Hit Counters don't need to be managed as they just increment on each web visit (you can reset the counters though). However, other Smart Objects, such as Blogs, Mailing lists, Polls, and Shout boxes will contain articles, an email address list, poll results, and a chat messaging log, respectively.

To manage a Smart Object from your library:

1. Click the **Smart Object Tool** button on the Web Objects toolbar and login.
2. Select the object from the My Smart Objects Library pane.
3. In the adjacent window, select the Manage... button under the object preview. The next step depends on the object type, i.e.

Object type	Reason for object management	How?
Blog	Adding, editing or deleting articles. Deleting comments from articles as Webmaster is also possible.	• Click the **New** button to add an article. • Click the **Edit** button to edit an existing article in your blog. • Click the **Delete** button to delete an existing article in your blog. • Click the **Comments** button to access a Manage Blog dialog. To remove a comment, select it and click the **Delete** button.
Mailing List	Removing a web visitor's email address.	• Select an entry and press the **Delete** key.
Poll	Zero the votes for a specific voting option or reset entire poll.	• Click the **Click here to zero the votes for this option** link or click the **Reset All** button.
Shout Box	Removal of unwanted text lines.	• Select an entry and press the **Delete** key.

To manage a Smart Object directly over the Internet:

- Login to **serifwebresources.com** to control your blog, polls, counters, and shout boxes independent of your WebPlus project. Use your usual Web Resources login as before.

Deleting Smart Objects

To delete an object from the library:

- Select the object's entry in the My Smart Objects Library pane and click the **Delete** button. A confirmation message is displayed.

This will cause any uploaded web page which includes the object to display an empty space until the object is removed from the corresponding WebPlus's web page and the web site uploaded again.

To delete an object on your page:

- Select the object and press the **Delete** key.

RSS feeds

What is an RSS feed?

Really Simple Syndication (RSS) feeds are streams of constantly changing news and information which are becoming increasingly popular on fast-paced web sites. The popularity of RSS feeds is evident if you use Internet-based news services regularly. You simply can't get away from them. The obvious attraction is the real-time update of information but an additional attraction is the ability to subscribe to these feeds and include them on your very own web page. You can see ever-changing content from many feeds all on one page—saving time-consuming site to site navigation!

You may have guessed that WebPlus lets you subscribe and place any third-party RSS feed on your WebPlus web page. However, WebPlus also supports creation of your very own RSS feeds—take control of a fast-paced information resource to benefit your web visitors.

Browser support for RSS feeds

As an emergent technology, RSS feeds are only be viewable in the latest versions of Internet browsers. Here is a simple list outlining browsers and their versions which can read an RSS feed within its own browser (with no third-party plug-ins required).

- Internet Explorer 7.0 (or later)

- Opera 8.0 (or later)

- Netscape Browser 8.1 (or later)

If you are using a previous version of the above don't worry! There are a range of RSS feed readers available via the Internet (type "RSS reader" into your favourite search engine) which will work equally well. A good candidate is the **Lektora** feed reader, fully integrated with Internet Explorer 6.0 and Firefox 1.5. Others include **Newz Crawler**, **FeedDemon** and **Awasu**.

Creating your own RSS feed

If you want to create your own RSS feed then WebPlus fits the bill. The **RSS Feed Tool** enables you to create one or more news feeds, which will be accessible to web visitors to your site. Stories can be added and appended to each news feed as you update it. Headlines, story summaries and supporting URL links are associated with each story. To update the feed you need to republish your web site (see **Publishing to the World Wide Web** on p. 211).

Here's a wildly optimistic "***Good Times***" news feed, to illustrate the creation of your own feed.

Income tax slashed - 10% off beer and wine.

Central government knock 2% off the base rate. To celebrate, a 10% reduction in beer and wine is announced from midnight. Cheers!!!!

06/06/2006 10:14 AM

Rush hour traffic declines..

Surveys suggest that commuting time in the countries largest cities have dropped by 5% yearly over the last 3 years.

06/06/2006 10:14 AM

Global warming - no evidence.

Antarctic survey team member Bill Stevens confirms that poorly calibrated equipment was to blame.

06/06/2006 10:14 AM

To insert an RSS feed:

1. Click the **RSS Feed Tool** button on WebPlus's Web Objects toolbar. OR

   Select **RSS Feed Manager** from the Tools menu.

2. From the dialog, click the left-most button to create a new feed name—edit the name in the RSS Feed title box appropriately. Click the button again to create more than one feed name.

3. Select the feed name in the My Feeds box, and click the button under the Headlines box. This creates a headline article in the selected feed. You should try to make the headline concise and, of course, interesting!

4. Any headline needs a supporting story. Enter this in the Summary box with the correct headline selected in the adjacent box. Optionally, add a Story URL, especially if your story requires references to other web sites.
5. Click the **Insert Feed** button.
6. A cursor is displayed. Position the cursor on the page and simply click the mouse.

A button appears at the cursor position. Visitors to your web page can view the RSS feed by clicking on this button. They must have a suitable news reader installed (see **Browser support for RSS feeds** on p. 194), otherwise unformatted XML data will be shown.

To update an RSS feed:

1. Right-click on the RSS feed icon on your page and select **Edit RSS Feed....**
2. Add additional Headlines, Summaries and a Story URLs as described above.
3. Click the **OK** button (the Insert feed button will create another instance of the same feed on the same page).

The feed placed on your page is updated.

Using the RSS Reader Tool

Instead of creating you own RSS feed you may wish to subscribe to an RSS feed from another existing web site—a web page's content can be boosted by inclusion of a feed from any popular news service (Reuters, BBC, sport, etc.) or other information service (e.g., financial). Many major news and information services host lists of RSS feeds relating to specific areas of interest (geographical, entertainment, political, music, etc.) so it's just a case of copying the link for the web site's RSS feed and pasting it into your RSS Reader tool. Please bear in mind any terms and conditions in using a third-party RSS feed—these should be clearly indicated on the originating web site.

Here's an example of an Investment & Markets RSS feed.

06/06/2006 08:42 AM
Smaller companies report: Monday close
UK small cap index closed a tad higher bucking the trend of its more senior indices, with Theo Fennell impressing

06/06/2006 08:42 AM
TUC wants AGM votes revealed
The TUC has called on fund managers to reveal how they vote at company annual meetings on behalf of their pension fund clients

06/06/2006 08:42 AM
Sunday newspaper share tips
Each week, we round up the main share tips from the

To include an RSS feed on your page:

1. Locate an RSS feed available on the Internet. Look for the XML or RSS button on the main web pages of popular news and information services.
2. Right-click on the button and copy the feed's link (in Internet Explorer, choose **Copy Shortcut**)
3. Click the **RSS Reader Tool** button on WebPlus's Web Objects toolbar.
4. In the dialog, paste the URL into the **RSS Feed URL** field.
5. Optionally, select a different colour, font, font size, or font style for the feed's Title, Headline, or Summary Colour.
6. Click **OK**.
7. A cursor is displayed. To insert the RSS Feed in a window of default size, simply click the mouse.
   OR
   More typically, to set the size of the feed window, drag out a region and release the mouse button.

The feed window will be filled with a peach colour with the URL shown—publish the page to view the current new feed. Remember that the content will change as the feed is updated on the original web site.

E-Commerce

Understanding e-commerce

E-commerce entails the buying and selling of goods on the Internet. It's difficult to escape online retailing in any Internet session these days—you've more than likely used some form of Internet shopping at some point, when buying online CDs, books, holidays, etc. Any web site that supports this kind of e-commerce activity will typically make use of a **shopping cart** system and a payment processing system. A shopping cart is n virtual basket (think of a supermarket basket) which stores your chosen items and is used in conjunction with a payment processing system (taking the place of the supermarket's checkout).

For major companies, the shopping cart technology is developed in-house (maybe the payment processing is carried out by a third party company). For smaller companies or organisations, the shopping cart is normally a brought-in third-party solution due to the cost/resource limitations. There are many third-party shopping cart providers that can be used—all account-based and equipped to accept credit cards instead of using a traditional payment gateway (e.g., by phone).

So where does WebPlus fit into all this? Firstly, WebPlus allows you to choose one of several specially chosen shopping cart providers and, secondly, it allows you to connect to the shopping cart provider via a form or link (i.e., a simple button or any object's hyperlink) on the WebPlus page. Forms allow for buying options (colours, quantity) to be set, as well as calculate tax rates, shipping, bulk items, etc. Links offer simple one-click purchasing without buying options. The features are provider-specific and as a result vary widely.

All shopping carts deal internationally - no additional files are need for this to work.

Configuring your Shopping Cart provider

A number of different shopping cart providers can be configured within WebPlus. These are the most commonly used and some, like PayPal©, you may have come across directly as an eBay© customer. The configuration process directs you to the provider's own web site from where you can sign-up as a registered user.

Use the provider's web site to find out more about unique shopping cart features.

To setup a site-wide shopping cart provider:

1. Click the **Configure E-Commerce** button on the Web Objects toolbar's e-commerce flyout.
2. From the **E-Commerce Configuration** dialog, you have two options depending on if you are an existing or new user of one of the shopping cart providers, i.e.
   - If you're a new user, choose a shopping cart provider by enabling its radio button, then click the **Sign Up Now** button. The provider's web site is shown in a new browser window from where you can register with the shopping cart provider.
   - If you're an existing user, enable the button next to your chosen provider, and click **Next>**. This option simply sets the default provider for your web site (rather than set up a provider account).
3. The subsequent dialog is provider-specific and may show offline testing options, window selection, store IDs, currency options and/or tax choices.
4. Click the **Finish** button to complete shopping cart configuration.

As an example, choosing PayPal let's you define a email address to receive payments, or use a "Sandbox", a test tool, for trying out your shopping cart before going live (otherwise you may start making money before you're ready!). Click the **Tell Me More** button to setup a separate Sandbox login in addition to your "live" PayPal login.

Once you've configured the shopping cart, you need to **Insert an e-commerce object** (see p. 201).

Inserting an e-commerce object (PayPal)

The creation of e-commerce objects within WebPlus takes a Wizard-based approach. An e-commerce object can be added to the web page as a form or link (i.e., a simple button or any object's hyperlink) by completion of a series of dialogs. Whether you choose to use forms or links depends on the characteristics of the items you are planning to sell, and how you want to sell your goods.

For example, if you are a trader wishing to sell a quantity of bricks you could create an **E-Commerce button** (as a Buy Now link). This option would make an assumption about the potential transaction, i.e. that all the bricks are the same style/colour and that the buyer would wish to purchase a fixed amount.

This is because a link is only a button and cannot host any "interactive" buying options that would be need for more complex purchases. One buyer's click will buy a standard product offering—nothing more. Useful in some situations but in others completely inadequate!

More complex purchases using **E-Commerce Forms** offer user interactivity coupled with flexibility. If we take the brick trader as an example again, a form can be used to host quantity and brick style/colour options so that the customer has control and can get what he/she wants!

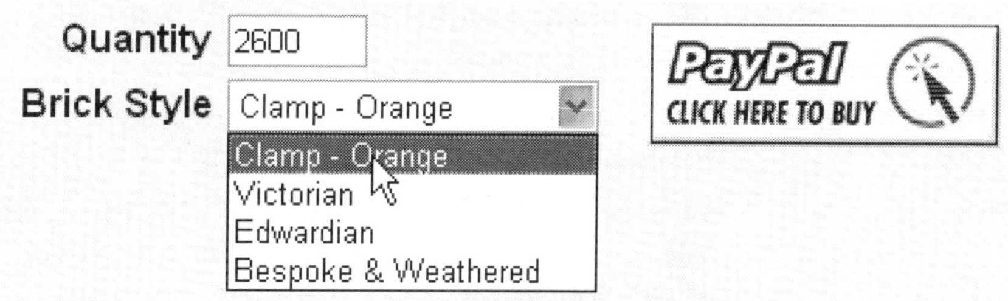

Here the web visitor has chosen to buy 2600 bricks of style "Clamp - Orange".

Form and Link Options

Forms	When to use?
Buy Now	When directing the shopper straight to the checkout. Up to two buying options can be defined. Form validation is supported.
Add to Shopping Cart	When the shopper is likely to buy more than one different item over the duration of a web session (and pay at the end). Up to two buying options can be defined. Form validation is supported.
Donation	For charitable donation is being made via the shopping cart. Form validation is supported.
Subscription	For subscriptions with configurable trial periods and billing intervals. Form validation is supported.

Links	When to use?
Buy Now Link	When directing the shopper straight to the checkout (no buying options or validation) via e-commerce button or object hyperlink.
Add to Shopping Cart Link	When the shopper is likely to buy more than one different item over the duration of a web session (and pay at the end) via e-commerce button or object hyperlink. (No buying options or validation).
View Shopping Cart Link	Use to check on your shopping cart from any point in your web pages via e-commerce button or object hyperlink.
Donation Link	For charitable donations being made via the shopping cart via e-commerce button or object hyperlink. (No buying options or validation).
Subscription Link	Subscribe to chargeable services or products via e-commerce button or object hyperlink. Single or repeating subscriptions are configurable. (no buying options or validation)
Cancel Subscription Link	For adding a Cancel Subscription button or object hyperlink.

Forms or links can be selected as radio buttons from a single dialog. Remember that the term "Links" is used because an e-commerce hyperlink can be made from a vector object, image, shape or text by use of this dialog (right-click on the object and select **Hyperlink...**). This would be instead of a standard PayPal button. See **Adding hyperlinks and anchors** on p. 149 for more information.

The dialog that is displayed when you add an e-commerce object will entirely depend on the currently enabled shopping cart provider (see **Configuring your Shopping Cart provider** on p. 200).

The following procedures assume that PayPal is configured as your shopping cart.

To insert an e-commerce object:

1. Click the **Insert an E-Commerce object** button on the Web Objects toolbar's e-commerce flyout.
2. In the Add PayPal Object dialog, pick the email address which is to receive the payment information. WebPlus will already assume that the email address set during shopping cart configuration is used. Alternatively, uncheck the Use the site default address box and set a different email address to override the site default.
3. Pick an object type from the PayPal Object box. Select a "Form" radio button if you want to create an **E-Commerce Form** which will contain buying options (e.g., colour or quantity). If the product for sale has no buying options then you can use a "Link" object (i.e., to create a clickable **E-Commerce Button**).
4. (Optional). If a Form or Button is not what you are looking for, enable the last option instead to paste code in a subsequent dialog. This would be code generated from PayPal's web site (look under Merchant Tools). Click **Next>**.
5. In the next dialog, define a button for use. It's possible to enable a standard text button (when enabled, enter any text string), a standard image button (when enabled, pick from an attractive selection of presets in the scrollable window), or load an image button (when enabled, use the **Browse...** button to navigate and select your image). Images are embedded in your site by default; otherwise uncheck the last option. Click **Next>**.

6. Item identification, pricing and tax information can be defined in the Item Details dialog (see WebPlus Help for details). Choose appropriate settings and click **Next>**.

7. For e-commerce forms only, the next step can be used to define user-selectable options (only two options can be selected per form in PayPal) if required. Check the **Add an options** field box and create a fixed name, an edit box, radio buttons, or combo boxes as appropriate—you can design from scratch or use previously saved options fields. Click **Next>**.

8. Set a default quantity in the input box, or check the box to let the user specify an amount at checkout.
   OR
   Set the Add Edit box option to let the customer define the quantity to be ordered.

9. For shipping and handling associated with the order, enter a set amount for the handling of the first item, every item or per order.
   If left blank, the default PayPal's profile will be used instead. Click **Next>**.

10. In the Extra Customer Information dialog, choose to prompt the customer for an address, don't prompt, or require the customer to enter an address. Optionally, ask a question of the customer in the text box. Click **Next>**.

11. The final screen offers some payment settings, i.e.

    - Enter the name of your Checkout Page Style (if setup in advance via your PayPal login).
    - Set a language for the PayPal login page. Pick for the drop-down list.
    - Change the text for the Continue button on the Successful Payment Page.
    - If needed, define Successful Payment Pages and/or Cancelled Payment Pages. Enter the page's URL or select an entry from the drop-down list.

12. Click **Finish**.

13. To insert the form or button, position the cursor where you want it to appear on the page, then simply click the mouse.

To edit an e-commerce form or button:

1. Select the form, right-click the form and choose **Edit E-Commerce Form...**.
   OR
   Select the button, right-click the button and choose **Edit E-Commerce Button...**.
2. Modify e-commerce settings screen-by-screen in the displayed dialog.

Adding options fields

The Item Options dialog allows for the configuration of up to two buying options—you can create form objects either from scratch or use previously saved default form objects. With the Add an options field checked, either of the two methods can be adopted.

Only one set of options can be configured per Item Options dialog. By clicking **Next>** on the first **Item Options** dialog, you will have the choice of enabling a second option on the subsequent screen.

To create a form object's options from scratch:

1. In the Option box, specify an object **Name** and a **Prompt** to appear above it.
2. Choose the type of form object required—Fixed, Edit Box, Radio Buttons, or Combo Box.

   - Fixed: Enable the **Fixed** option and add a name in the adjacent drop-down menu. Uncheck **Show on form** to hide the name from the user.
   - Enable **Edit Box** to add a simple box for data entry.
   - Enable **Radio Buttons** and click the highlighted **Add Option...** button below the window. Enter a Name and Value pair for each radio button option in the dialog. Check the **Disabled** and/or **Selected** check box to make the option unavailable (subject to script) or enabled by default, respectively.
   - Enable **Combo box** and click the highlighted **Add Option...** button below the window. Enter a Name and Value pair for each combo box option (click **Add Another** to build up your entries) in the dialog. Check the **Disabled** and/or **Selected** check box to make the option unavailable (subject to script) or selected by dcfault, respectively.

Radio buttons and Combo Box options can be edited via an **Edit...** button. Any selected option can be deleted by clicking the **Delete** button.

To save a form object's options:

- With the option for Combo Box or Radio Buttons enabled, click the **Save...** button. Give the saved set of options a name in the dialog.

To retrieve a form object's options:

- For a quick way of retrieving a set of saved Combo Box or Radio Button options, select the drop-down menu and choose the saved set. The options will be retrieved and will be adopted on the form.

Previewing and Web Publishing

11

Previewing your Web site

Previewing your site in a Web browser is an essential step before publishing it to the World Wide Web. It's the only way you can see just how your site will appear to a visitor. You can **preview** a page or site at any time, either within WebPlus (using an internal window based on the Internet Explorer browser) or separately using any browser installed on your system.

To preview your Web site:

1. Click the down arrow on the **HTML Preview** button on the Standard toolbar.
2. Select an option from the submenu:
   - **Preview in Window** (shortcut **Alt+P**) opens the site in a new internal WebPlus window with its own tab for convenient switching. (For details on using multiple windows, see **Working with more than one site or window** on p. 25).
   - Choose **Preview Page...** or **Preview Site...** to use an external browser. The names will reflect which browsers are currently installed, e.g. the entry may read "Preview Page in Internet Explorer 6.00". If you have more than one browser installed, you can select which browser(s) to display on the submenu. The page or site is exported to a temporary folder and appears in the specified browser.

When previewing in a window, you can use the Preview context toolbar to control the preview window. Click the toolbar buttons to navigate **Back** and **Forward**, **Refresh** or **Close** the preview window, and redisplay the page at one of several standard or a custom screen resolution (all from a drop-down menu).

To customize the list of browsers on the submenu:

1. Choose **Preview Site** from the File menu (or from the Preview flyout on the Standard toolbar) and select **Browser Preview List...** from the submenu:

The dialog displays a list of browsers registered on your system. The WebPlus **Preview** submenu will list these in the order they're shown here.

2. Use the dialog to make changes as needed:
   - Click **Auto Detect** to refresh the list automatically, or click **Add** to display a dialog that lets you locate a particular browser to manually add to the list.

- To delete an entry from the list, select it and click **Remove**.
- You can rearrange the list by selecting an entry and clicking **Move Up** or **Move Down**.
- To change the entry's name on the submenu or its path, select the entry and click **Edit**. For example, you could change "Internet Explorer 6.00" to appear as simply "IE6".

3. Click **OK** to confirm any changes.

Publishing the site to a local folder

Even though you may have saved your Web site as a WebPlus project, it's not truly a "Web site" until you've converted it to HTML files and graphics files in a form that can be viewed in a Web browser. In WebPlus, this conversion process is called **publishing** the site. You can publish the site—or selected pages—either to a local hard disk folder as outlined here, or **publish the site to the World Wide Web** itself (see p. 211). To review the basics, see **Understanding Web sites** on p. 19.

To publish the site to a local folder:

1. Double-check page name, file name, and picture export settings via the **Site tab** and **Format>Web Export Options...**. (See **Setting page and file names** and **Setting picture export options** on p. 55 and p. 129, respectively).
2. Click the **Publish Site to Disk Folder** button on the Standard toolbar (or choose **Publish Site** from the File menu and select **Publish to Disk Folder...** from the submenu).
3. In the dialog, locate the folder where you wish to store the output files. If the output folder specified does not exist you'll be asked if you want a new folder created when you click **OK** to finish the dialog (below).
4. Either check the **Publish All Pages** option, or in the site structure tree, check which specific page(s) to publish.
5. Click **OK**.

After WebPlus has finished exporting the selected pages, you'll be asked if you want to:

- **View site in browser**. This runs a Web browser to preview your pages—your browser is launched if not already open.

- **View this URL**. This option lets you view the site by specifying its URL, e.g. http://www.mywebspace3.com/intro/. For example, the publish operation could be to a remote computer's folder on the same network, where the folder is part of a web site on that remote computer and is therefore web accessible.
- **View files in Windows Explorer**. This provides a useful check of all the files published in Windows Explorer along with supporting sub-folders (for graphics etc.).

Publishing to the World Wide Web

Publishing to the World Wide Web involves a few more steps, but is basically as simple as publishing to a local folder! You can specify that all web page are published or only pages updated since the last "publish".

To publish your site to the World Wide Web:

1. Choose **Site Properties...** from the File menu and double-check export settings, particularly those on the Graphics tab.
2. Click the **Publish to Web** button on the Standard toolbar (or choose **Publish Site** from the File menu and select **Publish to Web...** from the submenu).

If this is your first time publishing to the Web, you'll see a Publish to Web dialog without any account information present (you'll see your local web site ready to upload). You'll need to set up at least one account before you can proceed.

1. Click the **Accounts...** button to display the **Account Details** dialog.
2. In the dialog, enter:
    - The **Account name**. This can be any name of your choice. You'll use it to identify this account in WebPlus (in case you have more than one).
    - The **FTP address** of your Web host will be a specific URL starting with "ftp://" as supplied by your service provider.
    - **Port number**: Unless directed by your provider, you can leave this set at "21."
    - Leave the **Folder** box blank unless directed by your provider, or if you want to publish to a specific subfolder of your root directory.

- You'll also need a **Username** and **Password** as pre-assigned by the provider. Most likely these will correspond to e-mail login settings. Be sure to enter the password exactly as given to you, using correct upper- and lower-case spelling, or the host server may not recognize it. Check **Save password** to record the password on your computer, if you don't want to re-enter it with each upload.
- **Passive mode**: Leave checked unless you have FTP connection problems. ISPs can operate passive or aggressive FTP modes of operation.
- **Web site URL**: Set your site's URL. This allows you to view the web site from a dialog after FTP upload.
- Click **OK** to close Account Details.

You can also use the dialog at this point to **Add** another account, **Edit** a selected account (for example, enter a new username or folder location), or **Delete** an account.

3. If you've set up at least one account, the **Publish to Web** dialog appears with the last used account name shown in the drop-down menu and its settings in subsequent boxes. The drop-down menu lets you swap to another account. Select the account you want to use (if you've more than one).
4. Choose which pages you want to upload—check specific page(s) in the window or **Publish All Pages**. Use the **Toggle Select**, **Toggle Branch** and **Select All** buttons to aid page selection.
5. To safeguard your WebPlus project, check the **Backup the document to the remote server** option. If the project is unsaved you'll be prompted to save it.
6. Click **OK**. WebPlus seeks an Internet connection, then:

7. If uploading for the first time, selected files will be uploaded directly.
   OR

   If uploading to an existing site, an Uploading Files dialog is displayed showing local file action (whether files will be added (Add), will replace the live file (Replace) or not updated (Leave)).

   In the dialog, select either the **Incremental Update** or **Full upload** Button. Choose the former to upload only files that have altered since the last upload. You'll see a message when all files have been successfully copied. Click **OK**.

8. You'll be able to see your page(s) "live" on the Web following upload. Use the displayed Web Site Publishing dialog to view the site in your Web browser to the URL of your live site.

Gathering server information

If you have an e-mail account, your contract with the e-mail service provider may allow you a certain amount (for example, 25MB) of file space on their server where you can store files, including the files that comprise a Web site. Or you may have a separate "Web space" arrangement with a specialized Internet Service Provider (ISP). It's up to you to establish an account you can use for Web publishing.

The basic process of uploading files to a server is quite simple, as outlined above... but some providers do a better job than others of "providing" the basic information you'll need the first time you publish to their server. Check your provider's Web site for the details listed below. (Note that Serif is not your service provider, and cannot supply the details you'll need.)

Before publishing, collect the following information:

- The FTP address, which is the specific URL (starting with "ftp://") of the directory on the server where you'll be storing your files. On many services, your personal publishing directory is just your screen (user) name appended to a standard URL. If your account is with a specialized Internet service provider, or you're using a dial-up networking connection or some other arrangement, you may need to do a bit more research to determine the required information.

- The steps needed to connect to the server, whether via LAN (intranet) or Dial-up Networking connection.

- Your user name and password, typically the same as your e-mail login settings. Note that one or both of these may be case-sensitive.

- Any other special instructions noted by the provider. For example, a particular port number and/or subfolder may be specified.
- Whether the Web server can accommodate spaces in file names. If you find it cannot, then choose **Site Properties...** from the File menu, select the **Graphics** tab, and check **Remove spaces from original file names** to revise graphic file names accordingly when they are published. (If you've already published your site, you'll need to do so again to fix the problem.)

Maintaining your Web site

Once you've published your site to the World Wide Web, you'll need to maintain the pages on your site by updating content periodically: adding or changing text, pictures, and links. Making the content changes is easy enough—all the originals are right there in one project!

Each time you publish one or more pages to a local folder or to the Web, a whole new set of image files is generated (duplicate .HTML file names are overwritten). GIF and JPG files can proliferate, and you'll need to weed out the old ones periodically.

- Within local folders, one method is to sort your Explorer or My Computer window contents by date, then use the "Modified" attribute to determine which files to keep (i.e., the set most recently published). For thorough cleanup, periodically publish the whole site to a new folder and delete the old one.
- To perform "housekeeping" tasks like file/folder deletion and renaming on your published Web site, you can use the WebPlus **Site Maintenance** feature.

To maintain files and folders on your Web site:

1. Choose **Publish Site** from the File menu and select **Maintain Web Site...** from the submenu. The Account Details dialog appears.
2. Select your FTP account name (from the drop-down menu), your Username and Password. Type the correct path in the Folder box, if required by your provider.
3. Click **Maintain**.

WebPlus seeks an Internet connection and displays a dialog showing the navigable web site's folders in a left-hand window and any selected folder's contents in the adjacent window.

1. Use standard Windows Explorer conventions to perform maintenance tasks:

- Click on the column headers to change the current sort order, or drag to change the column width.
- The top row of buttons lets you view up one level, create a new folder, delete a selected item, upload/download a file, and refresh the windows.
- Right-click to **Open**, **Download**, **Delete**, or **Rename** any file or folder.
- You can **Ctrl**-click to select multiple files or **Shift**-click to select a range of files.
- To move one or more selected files, drag them into the destination folder.
- To delete the entire web site, click the **View** button next to your selected Serif Manifest file—in the dialog, click the **Delete all managed files** button.

Remember to use the lower information window which displays a running log of each maintenance task and its status.

2. When you're done, click the window's **Close** button to terminate the FTP connection and return to WebPlus.

Index

Notes

Notes

Notes

Notes

Notes

Notes

Notes